Stronger Thar

D0503537

Stronger Than That

A Domestic Violence Survivor Uncovers the Truth About Her Abuser

SARAH DOUCETTE

Exposit

Jefferson, North Carolina

ISBN (print) 978-1-4766-9046-9
ISBN (ebook) 978-1-4766-4895-8

Library of Congress and British Library
cataloguing data are available

Library of Congress Control Number 2022035581

© 2022 Sarah Doucette. All rights reserved

*No part of this book may be reproduced or transmitted in any form
or by any means, electronic or mechanical, including photocopying
or recording, or by any information storage and retrieval system,
without permission in writing from the publisher.*

Front cover illustration by Anna Ismagilova (Shutterstock)

Printed in the United States of America

Exposit is an imprint of McFarland & Company, Inc., Publishers

Exposit
*Box 611, Jefferson, North Carolina 28640
www.expositbooks.com*

Table of Contents

Prologue

"Mom, Stephen is dead."

The phone feels heavy in my hand. I'm dizzy and I need to sit down, but for some reason I can't.

"What?" My mother sounds confused. I can hear people laughing and talking animatedly around her.

"Carol just called me. They found his body in the woods. They said it's either homicide or suicide," my voice cracks.

I pace the living room floor as I talk. I live alone in a third-floor walk-up in small coastal city in Maine. The apartment is quiet, and my voice sounds loud to me. A February snowstorm is dying down outside and a single plow truck rumbles down the street. The world feels muffled and claustrophobic. It's too cold to go outside and walk it off. I needed to talk to someone. Out of instinct I grabbed my cell and called my mother. She and my father are away in Texas for a cousin's wedding.

"I can't really talk right now. We're about to head out for dinner with everyone. I'll call you back later ... or maybe tomorrow and we can talk more about this," she says.

I stop pacing, sit down, and hold the phone in my lap. Why did I call? For some reason I feel guilty. I stare at the phone, feeling completely alone, more alone than before I called. But then it was always like this with Stephen. Feeling alone was the default setting. Those years I couldn't or felt I shouldn't share anything about our lives together. It wasn't fair to others. How could I expect anyone to understand? This was the kind of shock better absorbed on my own. I'm considering hanging up and then I hear her voice.

"Wait. You're upset about this and you need to talk to your mother." She sounds oddly flat, like she's going through the motions of being human. I realize she's in shock as well.

I hear her address the people around her. "Everyone, Sarah is on the phone. Her ex-husband is dead, and she needs to talk to her mother. I will join you downstairs as soon as I can."

Oh, God, now everyone knows. I hear my Aunt Wanda in the background. "What!? How does she know he is dead?" Of course it's Aunt Wanda asking this peculiar question.

My mother says into the phone, "How do you know he's dead?"

"His mother just called and told me."

I can hear my mother, raising her voice, addressing the room again, "His mother called and told Sarah."

I can't make out what they're saying but I can feel the shared shock in the room and hear a cloud of sound. I wasn't ready to tell the world about this. I just wanted it to be between Mom and me until I could reason it out. I wanted support, not an audience.

Finally, it quietens down as they all leave the room. Now we can talk.

We try to figure out what the cause of his "death in the woods" could possibly be. Was it a homicide or a suicide? I keep thinking how morbid this all is. It feels surreal. We're talking about my ex-husband as if we're on a CSI show. A man I lived with for six years.

"When did this happen?"

"I don't know. They just called me." My mom is asking me questions I don't have answers to. Questions I want answers to myself. The reality is starting to set in, and I want to cry.

"Well, what did his mother say?"

"She told me that his father went to look for him after he didn't come back from a hike. When his father got to where Stephen went hiking, he arrived at a crime scene with police all over the place and the officers asked him who he was. When he said his name was Roger Jones they asked if he knew a Stephen Jones. Roger told them that was his son and they explained that a hiker had found Stephen's body and at this time they are investigating it as either homicide or suicide."

"Oh my God, Sarah. What do you think? Do you think he would kill himself?"

"I don't think so. I mean, he never seemed depressed. And as mean as this sounds, he didn't love anything in this world as much as he loved himself."

"Sarah, this is crazy ... but is it not too far-fetched to believe that he would upset someone enough that they would want to kill him?"

Maybe someone did kill him. My mom was right. Stephen could be more than abrasive, and I knew he had done things that might drive someone to violence. Eventually we both came to that uncomfortable moment: are we truly sad about this? As horrible as this must be for his family, was this truly a bad thing?

Isn't this what we always wanted, Stephen to be out of our lives forever?

ONE

"A force for good"

A year went by. I was ready to forget him and everything about him. But while my mind knew Stephen was no longer a threat, my body didn't. When I saw a Jeep that looked like Stephen's, it still made me catch my breath and the back of my neck prickled, as if I had a near-miss car accident. Nightmares tormented me, routine chores could cause sudden panic attacks, and dating was filled with unforeseen terrors.

It felt like I was being haunted. What else do you call it when someone is dead, but you still feel their presence everywhere? In addition, I didn't know why I was being haunted. I had a sense I had dodged something very dangerous, but I wasn't clear on exactly what. Sometimes I tried to go back and figure out why I felt this way, but entire months were wiped from my memory. My memory for recent events was completely reliable, but much of those years with Stephen were either hazy or missing.

When I got a late-night call from my old friend Carrie, I didn't know what to expect.

"Sarah, I wasn't sure if I should call you about this. I don't want to open up any old wounds."

Immediately, I knew she was referring to Stephen. After he died, I Googled him several times. I was curious about his death. Maybe subconsciously reassuring myself that he was gone. I knew by then he had died by suicide, but I didn't know why. All I could find was a mugshot and criminal charges: "Felony Grand Larceny of >150K" and "Felony Swindling." I hadn't told anyone what I found, so I figured she was going to share something along those lines.

"Carrie, I'm good. You can tell me whatever it is." I heard her take a breath.

"OK, well, are you connected with my ex on LinkedIn?"

"No, I'm not. I'm not even sure I remember his last name." I thought back.

"You need to go look up his profile. He's written an article and published it there about your ex-husband."

This was not what I expected her to say. My mind shifted. I listened to Carrie talk, and at the same time, I wondered what Nick, of all people, could have to say about Stephen. It didn't make sense. She reminded me of Nick's last name, and I found the article, titled "How Do You Deal with the Suicide of a Mentor?" Nick wrote about having dinner at our house in Massachusetts, his memories of meeting me, and what it was like to work with Stephen. He described Stephen as someone who was important to him, someone who had shown him the way, a mentor. As I read the words and listened to Carrie, my heartbeat quickened.

Carrie said Nick had researched Stephen's crimes, meaning he knew things that I didn't about what happened. Things I wanted to know. I read on, my anticipation and nervousness building. He gave detailed descriptions of the crimes my ex had committed, but immediately after paragraphs regarding transgressions and felonies, he wrote about how he didn't care about any of that or what people said about Stephen.

"Stephen was a force for good in this world. Stephen had a bigger than life personality and left an impression on everyone he met. No matter what anyone said," he wrote.

Those words pinged around my brain after reading them. So should we forget his victims because he is dead? Because he's gone, he is absolved of all his sins? Because he was nice to you, he is innocent? But was Stephen nice to Nick? I knew that Nick wanted nothing to do with Stephen when they worked together.

My face got hot as I read through the article, my heart beating faster with every word. By the time I finished, my hands shook with adrenaline. Or perhaps it would be more accurate to call it rage. Even after death, Stephen's long con continued. My anger only increased when I read the many comments people left in response to the article. Seeing this outpouring of sympathy for poor Nick, who lost a dear friend and mentor, was almost too much for me to take. I thanked Carrie for pointing the article out to me and we got off the phone.

I sat in bed reading it over and over. With each reading I felt worse, but I couldn't stop. Nick's words felt like a slap in the face. It was as if he had stolen my story, my reality, and made it his own. I couldn't figure out why he would write something like this. What was the purpose? I kept circling back to the same thoughts. Do I say something, or do I just let it go like I always do when someone talks about how great Stephen was? I always felt like I needed to "take the high road" about such things and keep my mouth shut. But why? What was I afraid of? Why was I afraid of the world finding out who Stephen really was behind closed doors? Was I protecting his family in some way? Or was I protecting myself? Was I ashamed of being made a fool of? Or was I afraid of what I might find if I peeled back years of unconscious forgetting and hidden memories? Whatever my reasons for keeping quiet, something changed in me that night. I wasn't going to keep silent any longer. I was finally ready to tell the truth. Stephen was a monster.

I needed to respond to Nick. As I tried to formulate my long-dormant thoughts, I typed furiously and then deleted my words just as quickly. Finally, I was speaking my truth. I wanted to be firm but not mean or aggressive. Nick was lying, but he didn't deserve to be on the receiving end of years of pent-up emotions. I wrote six notes to him and deleted them all. Each note reflected a different layer of anger. With each draft, I got to a more rational and truthful place. After what felt like hours, I posted a comment of my own.

"Hello Nick, this is Stephen's ex-wife. I can assure you that after suffering years of abuse from him, he was not a force for good in this world. I also know that you were not his friend, as you and your girlfriend told me you hated Stephen when I asked why you wouldn't hang out with us. So, I don't know if you wrote this article to get attention or to get sympathy but please do not use my life to get those things."

My heart felt like it was about to pound right out of my chest, but I had done it. The truth was out. Just because he was dead did not mean he was now a saint. I closed my laptop, tried to calm down and fall asleep. I worried about how my message would be received. I knew I had done the right thing for me, but what would the fallout be? Not everyone wanted the truth. Maybe Nick was a person who preferred fantasy over reality? After what felt like hours, I gave up on the silly notion of sleep, turned over, and opened my laptop to see if there was a response.

Sure enough, there was a private message from Nick. My heart once again started to race; I was so nervous to see what he'd written. My fingers hovered over the link. I took a deep breath and opened my inbox on LinkedIn. I noticed that it had only been five minutes since I posted my comment that he replied to me. The speed of his reply made me think he was mad at me for calling him out in front of his network. I opened the message.

"Hi Sarah. I deleted the article. I'm so sorry my words hurt you. I should have deleted it a long time ago, as many others reached out to me saying exactly what you just said. People told me stories that shocked me. One guy, James, I didn't even know. A lot of people must have been looking for information about Stephen, otherwise how did they find my article? They all said the same thing though. Stephen was basically a horrible person, and I should pay more attention to the things he did, not just my memories of his mentorship."

We wrote back and forth briefly, and I asked him how he knew all the details about Stephen's crimes. He told me that when he heard about Stephen's death, he wanted to understand why he would take his own life. Nick said he simply called the county sheriff's department and the police in Colorado. Both sent him all the public records. He shared a link to his Google drive containing all of the records he had been given. Reading through them felt like I was reading about a stranger. This couldn't be my ex-husband. This couldn't be my life I was looking at. He must have started on this path when we were together, and yet, I never realized how bad it was at the time.

Nick's article and the sunny spin he put on Stephen's actions made me realize that it was time to take back my story. For years I had let his parents say that their son was such a great guy and that his marriage just didn't work out. It wasn't his fault, and he was a good man. That was their version; it certainly wasn't mine. I have no idea what Stephen told people about why we got divorced. I felt like I had been robbed. A piece of my soul had been stolen by all the people telling a fairy tale version of events. Over the years, I told my story to therapists and that helped a lot, but one piece was missing. I was still in hiding. I couldn't completely heal until I stopped being ashamed of my past and finally told the complete, unvarnished, ugly story to the world.

After reading the police reports I felt like I finally had some tangible proof. I know that sounds like a strange thing to say, that I finally had "proof." But over the years so many people had denied or minimized my experiences, I was starting to doubt my own reality. Looking at the police reports, I thought, "people will believe me now." and then I had a second thought: *I will believe me now.* I only knew half the story, even though the story was mine. Now I needed the entire truth. It would not be an easy journey. There was a lot about the man I married that I didn't know. To know my story, I had to know his.

Over the years I taught myself to dissociate from the experiences I suffered while with Stephen. Gaslighting, where an abuser causes you to doubt your own memories and history, caused much of my uncertainty about my past. Sections of my life were behind locked doors, invisible to me. This could be a path towards discovery and coming to terms with what happened.

Instead of being in the maelstrom of Stephen's chaos, unable to see the entire picture for all the debris flying around, I would take a forensic approach. I decided to be like a detective. I would interview the people that experienced other aspects of Stephen and put together a comprehensive history. Once I had a complete picture, I might find closure. Thinking of it in this way suited my OCD nature; pursuing and writing the story would eventually lead to greater healing. If I knew what actually happened, I might find real peace and be able to move forward with my life.

Two

Prince Charming?

If I was going to learn the rest of my story, I needed to go back to the beginning. It wasn't enough to uncover Stephen's crimes or unravel the confusing half-truths and lies Stephen had told over the years. Living with someone who is casual with facts or manipulates reality to suit whatever they need in the moment can make you doubt your own sanity. I needed to reclaim my story, starting with my childhood.

I grew up in Maine, "Vacationland," where you can visit L.L. Bean for camping supplies at 2:00 a.m. and find a good lobster roll at any roadside stand. We grew up playing outside. We built forts, went apple and strawberry picking, and wandered the fields nearby for hours with my dad, picking wild Maine blueberries. Every week found us climbing rocks on the coast. I am the oldest of two kids, almost Irish twins at a year and eight days apart in age. We had what might be considered an old-fashioned upbringing. To me and those families around us, it seemed typical. Dad worked, and Mom stayed home with us kids. Along with raising us, she ran an in-home daycare.

Every summer we went to a nearby campground at Lake Pemaquid. My father would scour the pages of *Uncle Henry's* for a new tag-along camper or a new boat. He liked to tinker and was a mechanic turned engineer by trade, so he would buy something that needed work for a great price and fix it up for us to use that season. *Uncle Henry's* has been a staple of Maine life since the sixties. It was a less creepy Craigslist before there was an Internet. To this day you can find anything from a pair of Muscovy Ducks to a vintage Cabbage Patch doll in *Uncle Henry's*.

My brother and I were each allowed to bring a friend to the campground. We spent hours in the pool, playing volleyball, roasting marshmallows, and sitting on the shore. The shore was my comfort zone; the lake was not. I wasn't afraid of monsters. I wasn't afraid of the water. If I could look down and see my feet on the sand or cool smooth stones, I was fine. But swimming out to the float or jumping off a dock sent me straight into a panic. I dreaded people asking me to swim to the float and always felt embarrassed when I had to stay on the shore. The darkness of the lake swallowing my lower legs and feet frightened me in a way that was simultaneously overwhelming and frustrating. Fainting in the water was a real possibility.

There were plenty of other things to do at the lake, including teasing people from away. My friends and I continuously puzzled at how little people knew about Maine. The year my friend Michelle and I were 12 and 14 we met two boys from New York at the lake. They asked us things like "How do you get to school?" With straight faces, until we couldn't stand it anymore, we would tell them we took a horse and buggy or a sleigh. The memories of those summers with my family and friends are as clear as any movie I might have seen last week.

When it came time for us to go to school my parents decided that my mother would homeschool us. She stopped doing the daycare and started teaching us full time. We spent a lot of time with other kids in homeschool groups or doing sports with the local recreation department. We grew up in a very Christian home. We went to church every Sunday, my brother and I went to youth group one night a week, and we joined the Bible quiz teams each year. When I was 12 years old, my mother could no longer homeschool us, so we started going to a school through our church. It was a private school, part of the School of Tomorrow, a very strict religious self-accelerated education program. At this point in my life, I was shy and extremely introverted. I struggled to make new friends simply because I was not brave enough to talk to new people.

My parents were strict when we were younger. We always had fun, but there were a lot of rules to follow. We didn't listen to secular music or watch certain TV shows until I was about 17. I wasn't allowed to date until I turned 16. It was the late 1990s, early 2000s, so while all my other friends had boyfriends and went on dates as younger teenagers, I never did. My shyness made it difficult for me to meet boys anyway. Despite that, a few guys in school asked me out. I knew I wasn't allowed, so I always had to say no. Now, I wonder if missing out on this "ritual" of dating as a younger person affected my relationships when I got older. Younger daters' parents offer more supervision. They drive you to your date and pick you up after or even supervise if they are over at your house. I feel that gives you a safer environment to learn about relationships.

Stronger Than That

To clarify, I'm not blaming the victim here. Some people believe Robert Anthony, who wrote, "There are no victims, only volunteers." I don't believe that. Anyone suffering from domestic abuse is clearly a victim. But I have an almost forensic impulse to go back over my life and figure out why this happened. Many people have asked me how I let this happen to me. If I could go back in time and change just one thing, would none of the following have ever even happened? Later I found that many domestic abuse survivors go through this stage. If we pull apart the scene, the wreckage, the burned house, maybe we can find what went wrong. What could we have done differently? But the more research I did, the more I discovered about Stephen and about most abusers, the more I realized that he was not the norm. Yes, I was shy and naïve, but those are not bad qualities. Taking advantage and victimizing someone who has those traits is the problem.

For many of us, gaslighting starts when we are children. All parents are a little guilty of this. They tell us something didn't hurt, ask why we are crying, or say we are too sensitive. We learn to stop listening to our inner voices, stop trusting our own feelings and intuition. Later, if we become the victim of an abuser, we hear those same things and remember our families told us, "You're too emotional and you're overreacting." It's easier to believe the abuser when they say it. All of this said, the only person to blame for all that followed is Stephen.

By the time I was allowed to date, all my friends had already gone out with the guys I was interested in. It just felt weird to be passing the same guys around. I did date one boy for about a month my senior year of high school. He was nice enough, but by that point I really didn't care. I was leaving for college in Florida, and he was staying in Maine to work, so I ended it quickly.

I was singing pretty much as soon as I could talk. At home, my dad played guitar and I sang along with him to old country and gospel songs. At church I sang in the church band. I can still remember singing "Bullfrogs and Butterflies" during offering with my cousin when I was just six years old. It was my first taste of performing in front of a larger audience and I loved the joy I felt and the encouraging response from the congregation. Strange as it may seem, whenever I was singing, my shyness evaporated. Every year I participated in a competition at the Regional Student Convention in upstate New York. These competitions were where I really gained confidence in my singing. I competed as a soloist and in trios, both all-female and mixed voice, in quartets, both all-female and mixed. Over the years, I took first or second place in groups and third place as a soloist.

Two. Prince Charming?

Southeastern University in Florida wasn't my first choice for college. I was looking at schools in the Northeast in New York and Pennsylvania and in Ohio. My parents and I took a week and travelled to do some college visits and to do in-person auditions for music programs. I ended up picking Elmira College in upstate New York. Elmira offered me scholarships and I was ready to go until I got notification that my scholarship package had fallen through. With a tuition of $36,000 a year, I couldn't afford to go there. I was feeling a little defeated when my pastor gave me some brochures on Southeastern University. I hurriedly applied by sending in an audition tape as there wasn't time to fly down before enrollment. I got accepted at Southeastern and Heidelberg University in Ohio. For me the choice was either more snow or sunshine. I chose sunshine!

SEU is a private university. It was so hard to leave my home and go so far away for school. I cried most of the way down there. I was comforted a little because my best friend Michelle was starting school there as well and we had managed to get a dorm room together. My family and I drove down with all our stuff. Michelle flew down later, and we picked her up from the airport. I was so excited! My mom and I set up our room, my dad and brother pulled the bunk beds apart, and before long the room looked awesome.

I became even more excited as we toured the campus. It was beautifully landscaped with palm trees galore, fountains, buildings that looked like high-class resorts, a cool bookstore, and a great café. I was captain of my high school volleyball team and was competing in the Junior Olympics for the state of Maine, so I decided to try out for the college team, and I made it. Freshman year was a blast. I was in my first opera and my first musical. I was "discovered" by Dr. Mei Chen and encouraged to change my major from church music to vocal performance.

I began taking voice lessons with my instructor David. One afternoon he decided that we should run some scales to check out my full vocal range. We started in the lower range which was not impressive to say the least. Then we started to head up the piano. I remember not really paying attention to where we were and just mindlessly singing the scales. Then I looked over to check in with David. He was playing scales with one hand, but covering his mouth with the other. He looked shocked.

"I have no idea what to do with you. I have never worked with a student with such a high vocal range. I think what I will do is have you sing for Dr. Chen and see if she can recommend some music for us."

Stronger Than That

When I was young, my mother always thought I was weird because I couldn't sing along with the alto-range pop singers on the radio. His comments made sense to me, and it was a validation that I was a high soprano.

Dr. Chen only worked with vocal performance majors, so at that time I could not take lessons with her, but she agreed to listen to me and help us pick out some music. I was nervous and excited, but the next day I went over and did some scales with her and we sang through a few pieces. She didn't give me any feedback at the time, but she did say, "I have a student performing in Orlando tomorrow night in *Pagliacci* and *Carmina Burana*. I have an extra ticket; would you like to go?" I was shocked that she asked me, and I immediately said yes. She told me she would pick me up at my dorm and we would ride down to Orlando together. I left her office and immediately started texting my friends to find a dress to wear to my first-ever opera.

The next night Dr. Chen picked me up in her tiny Mazda Miata and we drove to Orlando. We arrived at the Bob Carr Center, found our seats, and then the lights dimmed and the curtain went up. It was magical. I had never been to the opera before, and I was shocked at how much I loved it. The music, the voices, the costumes, and the sets were all so perfect and, honestly, overwhelming. After the show we went backstage to meet the cast and congratulate her student. On our drive back to campus we started talking.

"How did you like it?" Dr. Chen asked.

"I loved it! This was my first opera, so I didn't know what to expect, but it was great."

"Well, if this is something you really love, I think that you could do that one day."

Not sure I heard her right, I dumbly replied, "Really?"

"Yes, if you think you would like to do this, you will need to change your major to vocal performance for next semester and I will open up a spot for you in my studio."

"OK! I just need to check with my parents, but I would love to do that!"

The next morning, I went straight to the registrar's office and changed my major. I then called my parents and told them the whole story. I think there was a bit of disbelief, but they quickly got excited for me. The next thing I knew, I was in an opera every semester. I was enjoying the college experience and having Michelle around. Between volleyball and theater rehearsals I even managed to make some friends.

Two. Prince Charming?

Sophomore year my parents let me have a car, and my dad and I drove it down to school. We got all my stuff moved from the storage unit I rented with some friends, and we went out to Olive Garden for dinner. We were just getting back when my friend Anthony called and wanted to hang out. Anthony was an attractive guy from Columbia who grew up in Lake City, Florida. He was one of the first people I met at SEU freshman year. He talked to everyone and was very friendly. We always ran into each other at the café at school and hung out.

When he got to my dorm room to pick me up, he received a call from a friend who wanted to get dinner.

"I've got plans with my friend Sarah," Anthony told him. I could hear Anthony's friend's voice.

"Put her on the phone." Anthony handed me the phone, shrugging and laughing.

"Hey, we're all going out to dinner. I'll pick you guys up," this complete stranger said.

I felt a little nervous and shy. "I already ate dinner."

"Well, then, you can come and have a drink while we eat. Or just have an appetizer!"

"I just got back, and I should get stuff organized. You guys go."

"Nope. There's plenty of time later for organizing. You're coming out with us." Obviously not making a request, he was telling me I was going. Not wanting to be rude, and frankly too shy to argue the point further, I agreed to go.

I gave him my dorm information. I felt a peculiar little thrill, like I was going on a mad caper that was completely out of my comfort zone and my usual life. A short time later there was a knock on my door. I opened it and there he was, a 6'2" guy with an athletic build and broad shoulders. His long blond hair was in a ponytail. He was wearing straight leg jeans and a red polo shirt with thin white stripes and Adidas sneakers. He wasn't traditionally handsome. He had a large, pointed nose that was slightly crooked, and his teeth had a little yellow tinge to them like he drank a lot of coffee. But he was smiling, and I could feel his charismatic charm coming through. I was intrigued and knew almost instantly that we would date.

He introduced himself as Stephen Jones and said, "OK, are you ready to go?" The three of us went to dinner at Bennigan's. Bennigan's is a chain restaurant, much like the one in the movie *Office Space*. There are lots of "conversation starters" on the walls: an old sled, a vintage tin advertisement for cleaning polish, a rusty horn. The wait staff wear suspenders with as many colorful buttons or "flair" as they can fit. We all had a good time. Stephen flirted a little and made a few comments about my big eyes. I felt self-conscious and flattered. I hadn't received a lot of attention from guys up to this point. The fact that he was commenting on my appearance and complimenting my eyes made me feel like the center of attention. I had never felt like the center of attention before.

The three of us hung out a few more times. Somehow, every time we did, Anthony found a reason to retire early, leaving Stephen and me alone to hang out. Finally, Stephen and I made plans without Anthony, and we hung out a couple times just the two of us. Looking back, I wonder if they planned this.

At this time, I was dating Mike, whom I had met during the spring semester my freshman year. We spent the summer apart as he lived in Florida and I went home to Maine, but in theory we were still a couple. We talked on the phone periodically and texted back and forth. My parents weren't supportive of the relationship.

One night Stephen and I were hanging out at a small lake downtown. It was a romantic spot in the center of town, a small lake surrounded by a stone path and walls, illuminated by beautiful streetlights. As we talked, he got me to open up about Mike.

"My parents aren't really thrilled with the relationship," I told him.

"Well, how do you feel about him?"

"I don't know. I haven't had many boyfriends, so I really don't know."

"You would know if you had romantic feelings toward him," Stephen counseled.

"I guess you're right. I just don't know what that feels like," I laughed.

"I should tell you now," Stephen said, looking at me seriously, "I want to date you. If you don't have feelings for Mike, you should break up with him."

I was flattered. Two guys want to date me? Never had this ever happened to me before. So I had to choose. I realized then I wasn't interested in Mike longterm and probably just needed a reason to break up with him. Here was Stephen, charming me and making me feel important and special. To me, the choice was clear.

"Call him right now," Stephen said. "I'll be your moral support."

"Now? That might be awkward."

"Get it over with; do it now."

"I'll do it first thing when I get back to my room."

"Give me your phone." He held out his hand.

"What?" I handed him my phone. He held it for a second and then handed it back to me.

"Call him."

Something about this felt off, but right there with Stephen standing next to me, listening over my shoulder, I called Mike and ended the relationship.

Mike became very angry and accused me of cheating on him. I told him that I didn't cheat on him and that I just wasn't that into him. I told him that I had made a new friend that I wanted to date but I wanted to break up with him first. Stephen stood over my shoulder smiling and listening ... almost laughing as this all went down. Looking back, I can see that this was all a game to him. Now I realize what a huge warning sign it was.

THREE

"It was just a joke"

The romancing began. He had a dozen long-stemmed pink roses delivered to my room. He took me out for dinner often, charmed all my friends in school, and bought me random gifts. I had never had anyone pay as much attention to me as he did. It was all-consuming. I didn't have time for my friends anymore; we only hung out with his friends.

When I met Stephen, he was everything I wanted to be. I was so shy and introverted, but I wanted so desperately not to be. I wanted to be able to go out and make friends, but I had such anxiety about meeting new people that I just couldn't force myself to do it. Stephen was like my shield, my protector. Everyone was drawn to him like moths to the flame. He had no fear of talking to people, and because I was with him, I would get into groups by default. It was amazing. I had a new friend, and I was going out with people and having a blast. I learned a lot from him over the years about how to approach people and strike up conversations. Some of his confidence rubbed off on me. He was always overshadowing me, which felt safe, because I was uncomfortable being the center of attention. This was a great situation, until it wasn't.

I was in a show called *Night on Broadway*; it had a lot of Rodgers and Hammerstein music and big numbers with lots of glamour. I didn't have a dress for the show, so Stephen and I went to a local department store and we walked around looking at dresses. I tried on a few, including a beautiful gold dress which fit me perfectly and was just the look I wanted. I loved it, but I had to be practical. My high school didn't allow dancing and we didn't have a prom. This was every girl's dream, to wear a beautiful evening gown and feel beautiful. I didn't really have a lot of money and the dress was more than I could afford so we left empty-handed. The night before the show, Stephen showed up at my dorm and handed me a large flat white box. Inside was the gold dress. I couldn't believe it. It felt extravagant, but I was swept away by his thoughtful gesture and generosity.

It wasn't all perfect. Sometimes Stephen did impulsive, risky things that made me uncomfortable, but his friends thought they were hilarious. He was the kind of guy that would convince his friends to do stupid and sometimes dangerous things just for a laugh. He was the life of the party, the guy buying rounds for everyone at the bar.

Stephen was a "townie." He had moved to Lake City with his family as a young child and grew up there. He didn't attend SEU or any college, for that matter. He loved music and played guitar, so right out of high school he got a job at Musician Central in town. He was really good at sales and was making decent money for a 20-year-old. When we talked about college, he said he didn't need the headache or the expense since he planned to make Musician Central his career.

In 2004, four hurricanes hit Florida. Lake City was in the path of three of them. Being from Maine, I knew Nor'easters, but all I knew about hurricanes was TV news footage of twisted trailers, flooding driveways, and sagging power lines. I knew enough to evacuate when the authorities said to. During the first one I went to my aunt's house. The second hurricane I went to my roommate's house in South Carolina, and for the last storm my parents wanted me to fly home as the college was shutting down for a few days. I asked my parents if my friend Stephen could come home with me. They said yes, and they bought us plane tickets. He was very pleasant with my parents, and we all had a good time.

I was excited for our first Valentine's Day together. My friend Gretchen had been recently dumped and had no date for Valentine's Day. She was big into music, so she helped me make a mix CD of love songs to give to Stephen. We had just finished the CD when Stephen showed up and surprised us with a blanket and picnic basket with food for three. I thought that was so sweet that he made Valentine's Day special for me and my friend.

The three of us hung out a lot that year listening to music and walking around campus. At first, I was happy with this arrangement, but soon it felt like the two of them were getting closer and closer. I would be in class, and they were hanging out without me. One evening he was being extra flirtatious with Gretchen, and I got jealous. He noticed the change in my behavior and asked me to step aside to talk.

"What's going on?" Stephen looked at me intently.

"I don't appreciate you flirting with Gretchen like that! You two seem to be spending a lot of time together and you are basically ignoring me when she is around. If you like her so much, then you should just date her!" I yelled at him.

"I don't love Gretchen, I love you." He said it so quickly and simply I almost wasn't sure I had heard him correctly.

He loves me? No one had ever been in love with me before. That was enough for me. All was forgotten. We hung out with Gretchen less from then on. His flirting didn't stop, though. He was always flirtatious with the female servers at restaurants. I didn't think too much of it, as it seemed a ploy to get better service and tables. But it did bother me occasionally. Stephen used charm and flattery to get what he wanted out of people. It's weird to look back at this and realize that I noticed his tactics when he used them on other people, but I was blind to it when he did it to me.

Two of Stephen's friends were a married couple named Charles and Elaine. I was having issues with my roommate at college and my parents agreed to let me move off campus. I moved in with Charles and Elaine at their apartment, not far from school. I got a job working for another one of Stephen's friends, Tory, at Ashley Furniture in customer service. I stayed in Florida that summer working and living in the apartment to spend more time with Stephen. Things were getting serious.

Stephen continued to shower me with gifts and sweet surprises all the time. He bought me a pink iPod mini for no reason at all. One day, I had been in school all day and gone straight to work after. When I got home from work Stephen was at the apartment. He had cleaned and made stuffed portabella mushroom caps for dinner. He was always doing kind things like that.

He wasn't always sweet. I'll never forget the first time he brought me home to meet his parents. I knew "meeting the parents" was a big relationship milestone. I was nervous but excited to see where Stephen grew up. That afternoon I went over my clothes to pick just the right look; I wanted to make a good impression. When we got to the house, his parents couldn't have been nicer. They seemed as happy to meet me as I was to meet them. Our backgrounds were similar, and the conversation flowed easily. They invited me to come worship at their church. It was going well, and my nerves were settling down.

At dinner everything changed. They were having hot dogs. I can't describe how much I hated hot dogs back then. I remembered going to a fair with Stephen. He thought it was hilarious that just standing near a hot dog vendor made me gag. We laughed about it for weeks. But now there was a hot dog on my dinner plate, and I didn't want to offend his parents. I also didn't want to throw up on the table, but I'm made of strong stuff, and I forced myself to eat the dinner. Across the table Stephen was smiling at me and laughing under his breath. I can't remember if his parents noticed he was laughing or if they assumed we had an inside joke of some kind. After dinner, Stephen started teasing me.

"Tell them," he said.

"Tell them what?"

"You know," he laughed, "tell them about dinner."

"What about dinner?" Stephen's mom leaned around the kitchen door.

"Sarah hates hot dogs." Stephen was bending over, laughing like you do when you can't stop.

"But Stephen, you said it was her favorite food!" His mother looked horrified.

"I know. But she hates them. She gags if she's even near hot dogs!" He slapped his legs, still wheezing with laughter.

"Oh Stephen, that's awful. Sarah, I'm so sorry. I can make you another dinner. Come in here and let's get you something to eat." His mother motioned for me to join her in the kitchen.

There was no way I was having his mother make me a second dinner. She was being kind, but I just wanted to die. None of this was going the way I hoped. It was awkward and strange and I just wanted to go home. I was angry with Stephen but didn't feel I could let it all out in front of his parents. I kept quiet while they chastised him for the "joke."

In the car on our way back to my apartment I tried to talk to him about what he had done.

"Stephen, why would you do that? That was so embarrassing!"

"It was just a joke. Don't be so serious all the time."

"It wasn't a funny joke. I feel bad for your parents. Worse, I was trying to make a good impression and now I feel foolish."

"Exactly!" he said energetically, like I just solved some big mystery or passed a test. "I was just trying to be funny to break the ice. I did it for you because I know it can be a lot of pressure meeting parents for the first time. Didn't we all end up laughing about it later in the evening?"

He was right. Later in the evening he brought up the hot dog fiasco and we all laughed about it. Did any of us actually find it funny, or were we all just trying to make light of an awkward situation? I honestly don't know. I wanted to believe he wasn't being malicious, so I bought his excuse. Embarrassing me became a little game for him. He often did things to make me blush and then defended his actions as being playful and funny. He would tell me that I was just too sensitive, and I got embarrassed too easily. Now I understand this is classic gaslighting. Years later I read that when your partner does something that feels "off," imagine your best friend doing the same thing. If it seems outrageous, it is.

We never really had a fight, though. When I was growing up, my parents made it a point not to fight in front of my brother and me, so seeing a couple fight was not something I was familiar with. I thought it was a sign that our relationship was healthy and functioning well. One day we decided to visit a local garden and bird sanctuary. We had finished hiking around the grounds and got in the car to head home. We were both hungry and decided we should stop for lunch. This was the first time we had what would become our most common fight.

"Where would you like to go to lunch?" he asked me. I gave it some thought and replied, "How about Panera Bread?"

"No, I don't feel like Panera."

I gave it some more thought and made another suggestion. Again, he said no. I asked him where he would like to go or what he felt like eating.

"I don't know, you just pick a place."

I listed every location in town, and he said no to each of them, one by one. Part of me was wondering if this was another one of his "jokes" and soon we would be laughing about it. But I was hungry and wanted to get to the punch line.

"OK, I give up," I said. "Just pick a place or maybe we just don't get lunch."

He got quiet. I could sense the energy in the car change. I was confused and frustrated. Why was he making this so hard? It's just lunch. I asked him if he was mad at me.

"Trust me, you don't want to see me when I'm angry, so just leave me alone."

I didn't really know how to take this. I reasoned with myself that he was being sweet by protecting me from his anger. I just looked out the window of the car and we rode in silence until he dropped me off at home. It's easy to see this should have been red flag number 95. Looking back, it's obvious he would set traps for me. He wanted an excuse to get angry or be "disappointed" in me, so he created frustrating no-win situations. I had no experience with someone like this and I was in love with the man. It was easier to look for what I had done wrong rather than face the fact that I might be dating a sociopath.

Three. "It was just a joke"

That summer he proposed on our one-year anniversary. We were married six months later, on January 3, 2006.

Leading up to the wedding there was a lot of drama with his family. Stephen and I rented an apartment together. His family, as well as mine, were very devout Christians, so living together before marriage was a big no-no. True love waits and all that. We got the apartment because it was available and in our price range, so we wanted to lock it in a couple months before the wedding. His parents planned to buy us a living room set as our wedding present but refused to have it delivered if we lived together before we were married, so I moved into the apartment alone and Stephen continued living with his parents. There were lots of fights and a lot of yelling between Stephen and his dad over this.

I had always told Stephen that I wanted to raise my kids in Maine. We got word that the music retailer he worked for was going to open a new store in Maine, and Stephen asked for a transfer. They approved his transfer to Maine and advised us that we would have to move just a few weeks after our wedding. He decided he needed a new car with all-wheel drive for the Maine winters. To do that he suggested we trade in my car and he would give me his car. His car was fairly new, a 2003 Honda Civic he had been leasing. He convinced me that we would both be making out well in the deal. We traded in my car to get him a brand-new SUV. My credit was very good at 780 and his was not so good, so I financed the vehicle with him as a co-signer.

The next day he came over to the apartment and dropped off his car for me. He said he couldn't stay as he needed to get to work. After he left, I went outside to check my "new" car and it was full of trash. I mean, it was as close to a dumpster with wheels and seats as I've ever seen. The trash filled the back seat so that it was spilling over between the front seats. There was old trash underneath the top layers. It was a smelly archeological dig. I didn't see how it was my job to literally excavate the car. It was five giant bags of garbage at least. He also had dirty laundry in the back seat and in the trunk.

I was devastated. He had built me up to be so excited about a "new" car for me, but I couldn't enjoy it or even fit into it with all the junk. He just dropped it off and then drove off in a brand-new SUV with a sparkling clean interior and that fantastic new car smell. I immediately called him and told him that he needed to clean out the car before I could even use it. He sighed, as if I were asking him to do something unreasonable.

"I don't have time. I'm so busy at work right now. Can't you just take care of it?"

I was shocked. "No, I am not going to clean it. This is your car and your mess."

Again, he gave me a hard time about cleaning out the car. The absurdity and unfairness felt overwhelming. I couldn't help myself and started to cry on the phone.

"I had a beautiful car in great shape and very clean. I traded it in to get you a brand-new car with the promise that I would be getting a new car as well."

"Sweetie, you know you're overreacting. It's just some trash. Not a big deal. It's still a new car."

I didn't think I was overreacting, but his saying that brought on a fresh torrent of tears. I couldn't understand why it was my responsibility to clear his garbage out of his car. Finally, he agreed to come over and get the trash. The next day he emptied the contents into more than five garbage bags. Later, I detailed it myself.

Now I can clearly see how odd it was. He felt his behavior was rational and normal and that I was the unreasonable one. This was just one example that I remember, but life with Stephen was always in an upside-down world. Asking him to do anything he didn't want to do was "too much" and I was "irrational." At the time, I didn't see where this would lead. Maybe I just told myself he was young like me, figuring adulthood out.

I didn't want to get married on a Tuesday in January. But my wedding date and location were out of my control. My mother insisted that if she and my father were going to pay for the wedding, it had to be in Maine. She wanted to make sure that her family and friends were able to attend and none of them had the means to travel to Florida. I wished that I had been able to get married in Florida where my friends were. Because we got married in Maine, the only friends I had at the wedding were my two bridesmaids who lived in Maine and one friend from college who made the trip up. We decided that we would get married over Christmas break. But Stephen's dad couldn't get the time off until after the weekend, so it had to be on a Tuesday night. As someone who is good at planning, who likes to feel that I am managing my own life, it strikes me as strange that I had so little control over my own wedding. It was just how I was brought up; I was always surrounded by people who asserted their will over my own. This was only the beginning. Before long there were lots of things I wasn't in control of in my life and in my marriage.

FOUR

"You're always so selfish"

The "honeymoon" was over as soon as it started.

We had an early morning flight from Portland, Maine, to the Dominican Republic. For years the Portland Jetport was undergoing construction, so what might have been the routine one month was completely different the next month. We arrived very early for our flight, not knowing what to expect, and Stephen was already on edge.

"We should get something to eat before we go through security," he said, looking around at the few places open.

"Sure," I said.

"I don't see anything here that looks good."

"We could go through security, then," I said helpfully.

"I don't think there's anything to eat over there."

"We could go through security, look around and come back if there's nothing." I didn't see the issue.

"We don't have time." He looked at my carry-on.

"We've got plenty of time. It's two hours before our flight."

"No. You packed too much. I told you not to pack so much. We'll get stuck in security and then we won't be able to get back in time."

I looked down at my bag. It was a regular sized carry-on, with a book, a magazine, my wallet, travel documents, some tissues, and a few pens. Did he tell me not to pack so much? I couldn't remember. I had never had issues with my carry-on before. Was there a new security protocol Stephen knew about but I didn't?

"Well, we don't have to get a snack. I'm sure there will be something on the plane," I offered.

"What if there isn't? Then we're arriving down there starving after lunchtime. I don't care, but you'll be hungry."

"I'm not worried, Stephen. But I'm sure there is something on the other side of security. If there isn't, I'll go back through and get us something."

"You can't bring food through security. Jesus, use your head!" He rolled his eyes at me.

Was I hearing him correctly? This was the first day of our honeymoon and my new husband thinks I'm dumb? I couldn't process that right now, as he was getting angrier with each suggestion. Every time he had an idea, I agreed, and each time I agreed, he would disagree with his original idea. I was in the upside-down world of the restaurant listing game and couldn't see a way out. Finally, we got through security and headed to our gate.

"It's going to be too crowded down there." Stephen squinted at the gate area.

"We could sit over here, then." I waved at a row of empty seats by a plate glass window.

"We won't be able to hear them announce our flight if we sit there."

"Well, then ... we should sit closer to the gate." I looked at the gate area. We were so early, there were only a few people there. "There's plenty of seats."

"Yes, but there won't be. And we'll be all crowded in."

I didn't know what to say to that. There was no reasoning with him. I chalked it up to his being tired from partying after the wedding and getting up before dawn to catch an early flight, although for most of us there wasn't much partying. We weren't old enough to drink, and I remember the bartender telling us that if we were caught drinking, they would throw everyone out.

Stephen had never traveled internationally before, so I told myself he was just nervous. Maybe he felt like he needed to know everything, and the pressure was making him cranky. I had traveled to London, Paris, and Ireland right after high school, so I felt competent and relaxed. Or I was relaxed until Stephen started creating conflict over the simplest things. I felt like I couldn't take charge and be the leader of our group of two because I knew that would irritate him even more. But we couldn't just stand here in the middle of the concourse for two hours.

"Stephen, it doesn't matter where we wait for the flight, an hour here or an hour there, it doesn't matter," I tried to reason with him.

"Fine, we'll do what you want," he nearly spat at me.

An hour later, the counter opened for check-in, and we got in line.

Stephen leaned over the counter and plastered the biggest used car salesman smile across his face. "See this beautiful woman right here?" He wrapped an arm around me and pulled me close to show her how in love we were. "We're on our honeymoon. Going to the Dominican. Is there something you could do for us?"

The flight attendant looked confused. "Sir?"

"You know, could you maybe bump us up to first class? It's our honeymoon!" Stephen did a half turn, as though he were delivering a line to a packed house at a Shakespeare festival.

"Congratulations, but I'm sorry, sir, I can't do that."

"Of course, you can. You look like you know how to pull a few strings." Stephen's voice was soft like velvet, but I could tell the counter attendant was immune to his charms.

"Unfortunately, we don't offer free upgrades."

"Really? Really?" Stephen huffed.

I touched his hand that was around my waist and whispered to him, "Babe, it's OK, we don't need first class." He quickly turned toward me and glared, his face turning red.

Stephen turned his attention back to the counter agent. "You seriously won't help out a newlywed couple leaving for their honeymoon? Other airlines offer free upgrades for stuff like this all the time! This is unbelievable. I will *never* fly with your airline again!" He was practically screaming at this poor woman. My face was bright red with embarrassment, and I just wanted to melt into the floor.

The flight attendant refused to engage him and just gave us our boarding passes and motioned at the person behind Stephen in line, who was understandably hanging way back. As we walked back to our seats, Stephen grabbed me by the arm a little too tightly, pulled me close and in a harsh whisper said, "Don't you ever embarrass me in public again!"

"How did I embarrass you?" I was completely shocked.

"Don't challenge me in front of people," he hissed at me, squeezing my arm even tighter.

"OK, sorry, I didn't realize I was questioning you. I just wanted you to know that I was OK in coach." He released my arm, strolled over to his seat, and sat down like nothing ever happened.

Now there were two agents at the counter. Stephen decided that he should be able to get the new agent to upgrade us. I instinctively reached out to grab his arm but quickly caught myself, remembering his scolding from a minute ago. Was this really the beginning of my honeymoon? I heard Stephen laying it on thick and the second agent typed away and then looked at Stephen. "It doesn't look like we have any seats in first class, but if seats become available, I can put you at the top of the list for two seats in first class, but the airline does charge a fee for upgrades."

"A fee? Really? It's our honeymoon! You can't waive a fee? I know you can waive a fee. You just don't want to." Stephen again turned to his audience, as if looking for support and confirmation. It felt as if everyone looked down at their magazines and books at once.

"Or maybe you really can't do it. Maybe you don't have the seniority. Is that it? You're just the grunt worker? Is there a manager I can speak to?" Stephen leaned forward again. "All I want is a simple upgrade to start my honeymoon off right. Is that really too much to ask?"

I felt as if at any moment he might shout, "Do you know who I *am*?" I had never seen him act this way before. Or if I had, I hadn't noticed it. I don't like being the center of attention and people were looking at me, as if I could stop him. I wanted to tell him to be quiet, but I felt trapped. I knew enough by then not to even attempt to reign him in. He would not react well. I didn't want to make a scene myself, so I just sat there blushing, smiling graciously and a bit weirdly, as if I thought his behavior was totally normal. I kept trying to give a knowing look to the counter agents when he wasn't looking. I wanted to convey with my eyes and face that I was sorry, that I understood he was a jerk, but I couldn't do anything about it. Maybe if I kept smiling, they would know that I was friendly, no matter what Stephen was doing. In my head I was screaming, "This isn't me!" Thank God that when we got to the resort, we actually did get an upgrade to a suite with a hot tub for the "honeymooners."

While on our honeymoon, we signed up for a guided four-wheeling excursion around the Dominican. We were excited! We rented a four-wheeler and he drove while I rode on the back. We were having a blast. At one point the guide took the group into a cave, where there was a place to swim. It was dark, and the water was not clear. My childhood fear rose up in my chest and I knew I couldn't do it. I am that person who screams bloody murder when a piece of seaweed touches their leg while wading in the ocean. I was absolutely not going into the water. I told him I didn't want to and that he could go with the rest of the group members who were jumping in. He said it was fine and he would stay with me.

Another day he wanted to go sea kayaking, just us by ourselves using a rental kayak from the resort. Of course, I was terrified that we would flip over. It was a windy day and the waves looked enormous to me. I didn't want to go. I decided to trust him and tell him about my fear of deep water, how I had struggled with it my entire life and that I was truly terrified to go out there. I thought to myself, this is good. He will know me better and we will grow closer. But that didn't happen.

He cocked his head and looked at me as if he couldn't believe what he was hearing.

"What is wrong with you? Why can't you let me have one fucking thing I want?"

"What?" Now I was the one who couldn't believe my ears.

"Why are you always so fucking selfish? Everything about you, Princess Sarah. It's a fucking kayak!"

Right there on the beach, in front of hundreds of people, he was calling me names. "You always ruin everything! I can't have one fucking day without you ruining it! Seriously, what the hell are you afraid of? Will the wittle fishies nibble your toes, wittle baby? I mean, Jesus Christ, grow the fuck up and stop being a selfish bitch!"

"Stephen, I'm sorry. I wish I could go, but I just can't. I've struggled with this my whole life. You can go without me."

"What kind of a honeymoon is it if I'm going by myself? You could do it if you wanted to. You just don't want to. You're selfish. Selfish, stupid bitch!"

The world around me was getting blurry and I had a vague idea there were other people on the beach. The sun was shining off the sand. My towel was in my hand. The hotel was behind us. There was a feeling that I needed to pinch myself to wake up from this "dream." He was still yelling; I don't even remember what by that point. My tunnel vision was getting darker. I couldn't breathe and I sank down to the sand.

I put my head down, trying to breathe, but I realized then that I was crying, and crying so hard that breathing was difficult.

He looked down and made an exasperated sound. "You have to be fucking kidding me. Stand the fuck up. You're making a goddamn scene! God, you are so fucking stupid sometimes. I can't even stand you right now."

Then he walked away from me to the kayak rentals.

Up until this point, I thought he had been so kind and protective of me. Hindsight being the clear vision it is, I understand now that wasn't true. But at the time, it felt like it was coming from out of the blue. It was like a gut punch, all the air forcibly removed from my body so suddenly I didn't even know what to do to get it back. I was trying to breathe in huge gulps of air but that hurt, so I just took lots of small breaths to get back to normal. This was the first time I saw his temper directed completely at me. I really thought he would understand, that he would never put me in a position where I would be uncomfortable. His cruelty was frightening. I felt as if I was on a carnival ride: up in the clouds, floating, and then it suddenly drops, stomach lurching up to your throat.

His acting that way in public made it a hundred times worse. No one said anything to us while it was happening. People just walked by. Some stared and I could feel others moving farther away. Everything was happening in slow motion, in my periphery. I think he felt he was so right and justified in his anger that even if someone had confronted him, he would have been shocked. I was, once again, causing all the trouble by being irrational and overemotional.

Thinking back on it now, I find it incredible that rather than being angry with Stephen, I was mad at myself for having this stupid phobia. My body and mind had bought into his worldview. This wasn't an issue of his being inflexible, rude, and clearly abusive but due to a flaw within myself. I wanted to please him, but my level of fear was much stronger than my desire to make him happy. I was tying myself in knots wishing I was different. I was blaming myself. Even while I was sitting there feeling dizzy and sick, I was terrified for him out there on the ocean in a kayak by himself. I kept watching the yellow kayak like a nervous wreck the whole time. Writing this today, I know more about narcissists and gaslighting. I understand how easy it was for him to manipulate me. I wasn't even thinking about my own safety or dignity, I was only worried about him.

Years later, I understood his behavior was a typical pattern of domestic abuse. There are several types of abuse, and not everyone experiences all of them, but most people experience different combinations.

The most common methods of abuse are economic, physical, sexual, emotional, psychological, digital and stalking. Economic abuse is when someone exerts power and control over a person through their finances. This could mean not giving their spouse access to money, taking the money they earn away from them, putting them on a strict allowance, or even stealing their identity. We are all most familiar with physical abuse, the use of physical force to control someone, basically to create fear. Sexual abuse refers to any act that impacts a person's control over their own sexual activity. Sex requires consent, even if you are married. Forcing sex without consent is rape, and coercing a partner into having sex or controlling their access to birth control are forms of abuse. Emotional abuse, sometimes called verbal abuse, includes non-physical actions. Threats, insults, humiliation and isolation are common ways emotional abuse happens. Psychological abuse is gaslighting, using tactics to make the victim feel as though they are crazy. An example would be when you react to inappropriate behavior from your abuser and they say something like "You always overreact," basically making you second guess yourself and your reactions. Stalking includes being constantly watched, followed, or monitored by your abuser. In this day of technology, digital abuse is a big thing. It includes requiring access to usernames and passwords, monitoring your social media posts and then using them against you, checking text messages or call logs on your cell phone, texting you non-stop, and sending sexually explicit photos unsolicited.

I wish this paragraph included all the ways someone can be abused but, unfortunately, it doesn't. These are just some of the most common ways we see power and control exerted. But on my honeymoon, I wasn't even aware that I was experiencing abuse.

At this time in my life, I was very concerned with people liking me and I did anything possible to avoid confrontation. I tried to do whatever I could to make him happy with me again. The rest of that day we did whatever he wanted. He was different somehow. He was more relaxed, and it seemed he loved being in control like that. The rest of the week I walked on eggshells trying not to set him off again. The last day of our trip, we ended up with sun poisoning and we were sick all day, so we stayed in bed, slept and nursed our sunburns. The next day it was time to fly back to Florida.

We got on our first flight from the Dominican and we had a connection. At our connecting destination, we found our flight home was delayed. At the desk, we were told we could get on an earlier flight if we wanted. I thought this was a good idea and I didn't want to hang around an airport any longer that we had to. Stephen was not impressed. Our bags were not going to be transferred with us so they would land about an hour after we did in Orlando. Stephen began making up a huge stink about how inconvenient this was for him. I believe he wanted to get something for free from the airline, like a voucher or credit. He was speaking loudly so everyone could hear and started yelling at a counter agent.

"You're incompetent! Get us on another flight and I want my bags transferred too! It's not that hard! What are you, stupid?"

At this point I stepped in. "Babe, it's not a big deal. We were going to grab dinner in town anyway. Let's just get on this flight and we'll get dinner with your parents and come back to grab the bags when they get to Orlando."

I said this to him in the softest and sweetest voice I could, while horrified by his behavior towards this poor woman. He turned and shot daggers at me with his eyes.

"Fine, we will do whatever the fuck *you* want."

Turning back to the airline employee, he said, "Put us on the earlier flight but make sure we do *not* have seats together!"

I was shocked. I felt sick to my stomach and confused as to why he was so angry at me. I was just trying to get us home with the least amount of fuss. The woman gave me a look of confusion and maybe even pity. I kept quiet. We got our seat assignments and headed to the plane that was already boarding. He got to his seat and, without a word to me, sat down and refused to even look at me. I still didn't understand what I had done wrong. I found my seat in a different row.

After the plane took off, I thought the entire flight about what happened and racked my brain for what could have made him so upset. I reasoned with myself that this was the best idea, us sitting apart. He would have time to cool down, and by the time we got to Orlando he would be fine. He was just cranky from all the travel today. Looking back at it now, I'm amazed at how my thinking was already completely molded to Stephen's point of view. I was in the wrong, not him in overreacting to a common travel inconvenience.

I think I must have dissociated to a degree at this time. The American Psychiatric Association describes dissociation as a disconnection between a person's thoughts, memories, feelings, actions, or sense of who he or she is. Dissociation can be caused by trauma such as an accident, disaster, or crime. But there is significant research supporting that domestic abuse survivors experience dissociation as well. It can affect your sense of identity and your perception of time. I believe this is one reason as time went on that I became increasingly unsure of my own experience. Stephen was adept at making me feel that everything was my fault. Every explosion was due to my inadequacy, something I had done wrong. It was a fun house mirror reflection of reality.

We arrived in Orlando, and he got off the plane. He didn't wait for me. I headed out to where we were meeting his parents and arrived just behind Stephen. We stood there, side by side, not saying a word to each other as we waited. I still wasn't sure what to say, or if I should say anything at all. I didn't want to set him off again, so I said nothing. As soon as we saw his parents, he flipped the switch. He hugged his parents and then put an arm around me.

"Thanks for picking us up! We had an amazing time."

He leaned over and kissed me hard on the cheek. I'm sure the look on my face was close to a lopsided clown smile. What was happening? His parents commented on the earlier flight.

"Our original fight was delayed. But I figured, hey, why not take the earlier flight? We could see you guys sooner, have dinner and just come back and get the bags. Not a big deal, right?" His parents were nodding and agreeing.

"I'm just good with people, you know? They didn't want to help us out, but I changed that!"

Where was the raging and silent Stephen? At dinner, he continued patting my leg, leaning close to me, putting his arm around me. It took everything I had not to flinch in front of his parents. My head was spinning.

"The place was fantastic. We went exploring and kayaking, and we had so much good food. The beaches were incredible. Just like in the pictures. We got sun," he laughed. "We might have gotten too much sun."

When his parents dropped us off at home, I wasn't sure what to expect. But he said nothing about the episode at the airport and nothing about his peculiar conduct at dinner. It was as if nothing strange had happened.

The whole next week was so confusing. I spent a lot of time thinking and reasoning with myself about what happened. I figured I just didn't know what to expect living with a man. I wanted things to work and to live "happily ever after," so I was eager to find explanations for his behavior. I just wrote things off as personality quirks. Maybe he just missed his parents that week? Maybe he was still suffering from sun poisoning? I explained it all away.

Five

"I care too much about you"

A few weeks after our honeymoon, we moved to Maine and lived with my parents for a brief time. My parents set us up with a private space in the basement. We made our own little world down there and didn't spend much time with them in the main areas of the house. Stephen worked late, so he would sleep in, shower, go to work and then come home after they were in bed. I barely saw him because he was working long hours to get the new store ready for the grand opening.

I was supposed to re-enroll in a music program in Maine but that never happened. Stephen talked me out of it. He frequently told me that I would never make it as a professional musician, that I wasn't as talented as I thought or as people at SEU told me I was. He said SEU was just a small private college, and no one cared what they thought there anyway.

"I care too much about you to see you get let down. Things would be different here. At SEU you were a big fish in a little pond. I don't say this to hurt your feelings, but you have to know you're just not professional musician caliber."

I brought it up a few times because I felt derailed from my life plan. I missed singing and the camaraderie of a music program. Stephen sat me down to "face some hard truths."

"Sarah, the thing is, you're just not good enough to ever make money at it, you know? So, if you can't make money singing, why do it? I hate to see you waste time and money on something that won't work out. I love you."

I believed him when he said I wasn't good enough for a music program or a career. Looking back, it's hard to imagine how he was able to convince me of this. I minimized my own experiences with Dr. Chen. I ignored my lifetime of singing. He wore away at my own reality like a stream of water wears down a stone. Soon my reality was warped and curved to fit Stephen's needs, not my own. What I wouldn't realize until much later is that he wanted to be the best at everything, and let's face, it I was better. If I had kept up with my music studies and lessons, who knows where I would be with my musicianship right now? He ended up never doing anything with his music. He sold instruments and learned a few riffs to show off, but he never played at home or had any true love for music.

Stephen could hide himself very well if you were only with him for a couple hours at a time. He tried hard to show me lots of affection around my parents, though my mother has since told me that she noticed that he wouldn't touch me often. You know how new couples will sit so close they are almost on each other's laps? My mother was expecting that, but it wasn't happening. One time we were playing pool in the basement at my parents' house and my aunt and her boyfriend were over. We all had some drinks, and I was silly and tipsy. Stephen was so annoyed and embarrassed by me, he couldn't stop himself from chastising me and giving me dirty looks, telling me to get it together. My mother immediately picked up on this. He scolded me for being silly and I sat down. She looked at him and said, "You leave her alone and let her have fun!" He made up some excuse about being worried I would fall and hurt myself. I was only one or two glasses of wine in, so in no way was I stumbling around; I was just loose and laughing and teasing with my family and making jokes.

Before we were able to find an apartment in Maine, he got a promotion from assistant manager in Portland to general manager of his own new store in Massachusetts. We found a place and got ready to move to Worcester. One day right before we moved, he came home with an expensive looking laptop.

"Wow. That's a sleek-looking laptop! Where did that come from?"

Stephen opened it up on the kitchen table. "Musician Central gave these laptops to all general managers since they have to do work at home in the evenings."

"That's amazing. I mean, look at the graphics!" The laptop was nicer than anything I had ever seen outside of a display in Best Buy. It almost looked like a gamer's laptop. There was a faint voice in the back of my mind saying this was weird, but I had no reason not to believe him. It was a reasonable explanation, so I let it go.

Once we were in Worcester it was shocking how fast things changed. We were five months into our marriage at this point. Stephen surprised me on my birthday with a trip to the ASPCA. We adopted two kittens, Martin and Taylor. I was excited to be a wife and homemaker. I had always dreamed of having my own place and doing things the way I wanted. I was playing house, I suppose.

There's a strange retro alchemy that happens when you get married young. Maybe not everyone experiences this, but at the time, I felt that marriage was a badge of adulthood. I wanted to do it right. A lot of my ideas were from another time. It was as though my nesting instinct had watched 36 continuous hours of *Leave It to Beaver*. I wanted to make my husband happy. I wanted a clean and functioning house. It made me feel good to do things for him. So, for those first months, I was happy to be cooking meals and cleaning up. I don't think I noticed right away, but soon the strain of work and bearing the burden of all the housework took its inevitable toll. In my household, I expected that I would do the cooking for the most part and that my husband would take out the trash and help me clean. When I asked Stephen for help, I was met with the rage of a cranky toddler being asked to clean his room. But a toddler temper tantrum thrown by a six-foot, 190-pound man is not as funny or easy to fix with a time-out.

I found myself annoyed with him as we fell into the following routine: Stephen went to work, came home, ate dinner, and afterward sat on the couch and played video games or watched TV. I was expected to go to my own job, do the grocery shopping, do the laundry, make dinner, clean up after dinner, clean the bathrooms, do all the other housework, and bring him drinks whenever he asked. Where was the man who surprised me with a tidied-up room when we were dating?

I was working for a sunroom construction company as an office and showroom manager. Later, I found a job as an assistant to the VP of purchasing for apparel and jewelry at one of those large club stores where you buy everything in bulk. I was working hard in the home and out of it. Anyone who knows me knows I've got energy to spare. I like multi-tasking. I'm good at juggling numerous responsibilities and keeping it together. But doing everything on my own while I was married made me feel more alone than I could remember ever feeling. It was as if I was the engine for the marriage, and without me pulling all the weight, nothing would get done.

I thought maybe we just needed to communicate about how things were, like a mature married couple. He had a habit of staying up late and making himself snacks. In the mornings, instead of finding my clean kitchen from the night before, there were baking pans, spatulas, bowls, glasses, wrappers, and crumbs everywhere. If he got home from work at night and the kitchen was still a mess, he would get so upset about it. So every day I cleaned the kitchen twice. I told him I was exhausted and needed help. Maybe he could pitch in with a few of the household chores? Maybe just clean up the kitchen at night after his snacks or put his dishes in the sink? He looked at me with absolute loathing.

"I work so hard every day and all you do is bitch at me about cleaning and cooking. You can never just let me be. You're always bitching at me! All the shit I do for you and you can't even let me come home and fucking relax."

His response was a severe overreaction. I just wanted to talk to him like married couples should be able to. I'm a very non-confrontational person, so this was devastating to me. I shut right up. Inside I was thinking, "What the hell? I work full-time and I'm expected to be the only one cooking and cleaning? This isn't fair!" It's strange how we rationalize these situations. Our relationship as a married couple was still new and I was trying to figure out his personality. I wondered if he was just stressed and I should find a better time to talk to him about how I was feeling. Or was his overreaction because of something else? I had no clue what it could be. All I knew was that he was mean.

Our routine continued. One night I was sitting on the couch watching a movie with him after having done all of the housework, grocery shopping, laundry and cooking and working a full day at my own job. He told me to go get him a soda from the kitchen. He caught me in a moment where I couldn't hold back.

"I am not your maid or your servant, I am your wife. Go get your own soda."

I had instant regret. He turned to look at me in slow motion, his face full of disgust and hate.

"You're a bitch! I'm fucking tired. I worked all goddamn day and I just want to come home and relax. The least you can do is get me a fucking soda."

The hate I felt coming from him made me afraid to say anything more. I wasn't going to risk an escalation. I couldn't imagine what that would look like, but I knew in my bones it wouldn't be good. He was on a roll, and I wasn't sticking up for myself, so he just continued.

"I've never met anyone as lazy as you. How hard is it to clean a fucking house?" He rolled his eyes. "It's like the simplest thing is too hard for you. You're the stupidest, most selfish idiot I've ever met. Just plain lazy."

I got the soda just to make it stop.

We stopped having sex about three months into our marriage. I tried everything to get him interested in me. I didn't have much experience in this department, so I tried anything I could think of from wearing lingerie to just walking around naked ... and nothing. He would rather lie on the couch and watch TV or play video games than be intimate with me. I had no clue how to handle this situation. Maybe he just didn't have much of a sex drive? After we got married, he was never affectionate. We didn't hold hands anymore or kiss randomly. I saw couples with their arms around each other, heads close together, and I remembered when we had been like that, just three months earlier. I was starting to feel like he married me just so that he could have a maid and a cook.

Since we were new to the area, we were trying to make friends. Stephen had recently hired Nick at Musician Central. Nick had a girlfriend, Carrie, and we invited them over for dinner. The dinner at our house went great. Stephen of course put on the charm; I typically refer to this "mask" as "The Stephen." He was warm and inviting, he was great at getting conversations going (granted, most of them were about him and some great thing he had done), and he was very good at making it look like I was the greatest wife and how much he appreciated me. I was so excited to have made new friends. This would mean that we could go out and have dinner or just hang out with them and of course that meant I would see more of "The Stephen." We went out to dinner with them twice and then we never really hung out again. I was so confused as to why they kept turning down our invitations to do things together.

Carrie and I, however, were still friends. We would go shopping or take her dogs to Boston Common, walk around and grab lunch. During one of these outings, I asked her why we didn't hang out as couples anymore and she said, "We really don't like your husband; he's really rude and embarrassing in restaurants." I knew deep down what she said was true and I really needed a friend, so I didn't push the issue.

Later in our friendship Carrie and Nick got engaged. I was so excited and happy for them. Carrie and I went to a local bridal shop together so she could try on wedding dresses. After her appointment, we were walking back to our cars, and she stopped me in the parking lot.

"I really want to have you as a bridesmaid in my wedding, but I can't."

I was shocked and confused. "I don't understand. Why can't you? Did I do something?"

She looked at me like I should already know why. "We can't have Stephen at our wedding. He is just too insulting and rude. He wants everything to be about him and we're afraid he'll ruin our wedding."

My heart sank. This was a really hard and awkward moment for Carrie and me. We both teared up a little. I assured her that I understood and that I wasn't upset with her.

Years later, when I read Nick's article eulogizing Stephen, about what a great guy he was, a mentor he looked up to, this was one of the moments I thought about. At that time, Carrie was one of my closest friends and I couldn't even go to her wedding because of Stephen's behavior. Nick and Carrie's reluctance to have Stephen there was understandable, but naturally, when I read Nick's "fond memories," all of my feelings around this moment came up again. My disappointment, sadness, and anger were as fresh as that day in the parking lot.

Around this time, I started to recognize some distinct "personas" that Stephen would exhibit based on where he was and who we were with. It was almost like he had different personalities. For each version of Stephen there was a different name, and he would sometimes use these names to refer to himself in the third person. I'm not saying he had a multiple personality disorder or some sort of identity issue. It was more that he had different "masks" he would put on for different occasions. None of them were real; each "mask" was Stephen play-acting at being someone else. He was being what he perceived "you" would want him to be. Basically, it was like a chameleon changes colors to match its surroundings.

There was Stephen, Steve, Steve-O, Superman, The Stephen, and The Stephen of Doom.

When "Stephen" spoke to anyone in public he never made eye contact. He scanned the room and spoke at a volume that would ensure everyone around him could hear. It felt like he wanted everyone to know how smart and special he was; everything he did was for show. The clothes he wore were more expensive than we could afford, so he looked like he had more money than he had. Our apartment was more expensive than we could afford, but our cable and electricity were frequently shut off due to lack of payment. But he had no problem buying a new pair of $100 jeans or shoes. This was his politician personality; I don't know of any other way to describe it. This was the smooth talker I first met on the phone that day. He was an excellent salesman. He was the top sales guy every month in his store and one of the top salespeople in the district.

His "Superman" persona was like "Stephen Plus." When going out to eat he would put our names in for a table and very loudly he would tell the hostess his name was Superman. He would do this while looking around to make sure everyone heard him and gave him a reaction of some sort. This embarrassed me and any friends we went out with. Then when the hostess would call out, "Table for 4 for Superman!" he would jump up and yell, "Yes, Superman, that's me!" and strut for everyone to see which again embarrassed everyone with him. In Florida he had a lot of immature friends that thought this was funny. When we moved up north, we didn't have many friends, as they could not stand this behavior.

"Steve-O" was the guy who convinced his friends to do stupid and sometimes dangerous things. The guy who bought rounds for everyone at the bar. The guy who towed his friend behind his truck on a skateboard with a thin rope and a scrub brush for a handle while another friend videotaped it. When the friend fell and got severe road rash, "Steve-O" thought it was hilarious. He just didn't have any regard for other people getting physically injured.

"The Stephen" was his sales guy persona. He would answer the phone at work "Thank you for calling Musician Central. This is The Stephen!" This guy was very pleasant and upbeat. He was high energy and very knowledgeable about anything in the store. This was the guy you wanted to be friends with and you trusted to give you a good deal on your next guitar. This is who I dated and fell in love with. In fact, after we were married, sometimes I visited him at work, just so I could see "The Stephen." I was friends with most of his co-workers and brought them home-baked goods, remembered their birthdays, and asked after their families. When I walked in, they would yell, "Sarah!" and give me hugs. Stephen would watch them, and it felt like he tried to outdo them. Or maybe he was taking a cue from how they treated me. Whatever it was, "The Stephen" would come out, and he was loving and affectionate towards me. It was the only time he was affectionate in those years. Now, even driving by the Musician Central makes me anxious.

I never understood "The Stephen of Doom." It wasn't that he was evil when he called himself "The Stephen of Doom"; it was more like he was giving you a subtle warning about what lies beneath without letting you see any of the true nature. This was his name on Facebook for a while, this was his email address for some time, and this was his gamer name when playing *Call of Duty*.

It felt as if Stephen couldn't sustain just being Stephen. The real Stephen, whoever that was. He always had to be changing costumes because he couldn't bear to be just himself for any length of time. Not that he would have identified that impulse in himself. His narcissism would never have allowed a moment of doubt or self-reflection. Now I think he used each mask to blend in with normal people.

Life went on. I was his maid and I continued to resent it. Every time I asked for help, he got meaner and angrier. Sometimes the mess in the house was like a natural force that I couldn't hold back, like the tide. Not only did Stephen not clean or help tidy up, but he also just dropped everything wherever he was standing. Shoes came off in random places, dirty clothes were left wherever he took them off, dirty glasses never made it to the sink. I was constantly picking up this sea of trash and things Stephen was done with. If he brought papers home from work, they were dumped wherever he sat down. But if I tried to tidy up and find a "regular place" for them, he would throw a fit. If I tried to vacuum or clean while he was playing video games, he became enraged. I had to clean around his schedule. From the time I got home from work in the evening to the time I went to work in the morning, I was holding back household chaos.

One morning the house was a mess, and he couldn't find his favorite shirt. I was still in bed. Sometimes it was easier to get up after he left and get ready in a rush rather than get in his way. Without thinking it through, I asked him what time he would be home that night. I needed to know because if dinner wasn't ready, there would be another blow up. My question lit the fuse.

"This house is a fucking disaster! I can't find anything in here! Just lie in bed and do nothing. You are so lazy and disgusting. I can't fucking stand to even look at you! I hate you!"

He picked up his dirty clothes from the floor and threw them at me in bed. I was stunned. I just sat there and cried under a pile of his dirty socks and underwear until he left. The door slammed, I heard his car drive away, and after I was sure he wasn't coming back, I got up. In a daze, I showered, dressed, and got to work. I cried at my desk until I just couldn't stand it anymore. I told my boss I was leaving, and I jumped in my car and drove three hours to my parents' house in Maine.

Once in Maine, I talked to my mom and tried to just cry it out. She set up her bed for me and I cried, trying to figure out who the hell I had married. We were only in the seventh month of our marriage and it was like he was a totally different person from the one I dated. Why was he so mean? I'm sure it was confusing for my family, but I couldn't easily describe how I felt. It was as if I had married a complete stranger. I could hear my mother in the kitchen talking on the phone with friends or family members about what was going on. "I don't know. She is here and crying and upset. She says that she and Stephen are fighting, and she may want to leave him."

I didn't know who she was talking to, but I hated hearing those words spoken out loud. Eventually she came into the room and handed me the phone. She said that my Aunt Wanda wanted to talk to me. Wanda was notorious for getting involved in or starting family drama. I wasn't sure I wanted to talk to her but my mom wanted me to. Wanda was divorced and my mom thought she would understand what I was going through. I took the phone and Wanda was being very dramatic and doing this "scolding advice" thing.

"Sarah, you *deserve* better, and you *need* to take care of yourself. *Forget* him! What did he do to you?!"

It was just too much from her, so I found myself making excuses for Stephen and his behavior. "He just gets so stressed out with work, and when he comes home, he is in a bad mood and we fight." I basically downplayed everything to get her off the phone. Even though Wanda was trying to be encouraging, her words increased my feelings of failure. They got to that part of me that Stephen had already changed, the part that believed everything was my fault. How could I be thinking of divorce just a few months into my marriage? Clearly, I was an abject failure.

My mind was all over the place. I was relieved to be out of that apartment with the new "angry all the time Stephen," but weirdly, I started to stress about having to date if we got divorced. I made a mistake when I talked about this with my mother. It felt as though she now thought I wasn't serious about divorce and that I was just having fun thinking about dating since I had only dated one other person before Stephen. Looking back, I feel this removed some of the seriousness of my complaints. She felt like I had no business talking about dating and I needed to focus on my marriage. My mother contacted an attorney friend who stopped by and talked to us about getting an annulment versus a divorce. I was so overwhelmed I have no clue what she even said to me.

When he got home and I wasn't there, the phone calls, text messages, and voicemails started pouring in. The vilest, most poisonous things were said.

"Where the hell are you?" he texted me.

"I am at my parents' house."

My phone immediately rang. "Hello."

"You are a fucking coward! Get your ass back home and talk to me face to face like a fucking adult. Only fucking babies go running home crying to mommy and daddy. No one can respect someone who runs away!"

I hung up the phone. For three days I stayed in Maine refusing to answer his calls and text messages. Eventually, he calmed down and sent some messages that indicated that he might be calm enough to talk. We spoke on the phone, and he promised to work on his temper. He promised to help me around the house. He apologized for everything and told me how much he loved me. Everything I wanted to hear, he said, and I believed him, so I went back.

Now I know that it takes an average of seven times for a partner to leave an abusive relationship. I still didn't know I was experiencing abuse. With the benefit of knowledge and hindsight, it's hard for me to imagine that I didn't see the daily yelling, name calling, threats, games, and cruelty as abuse. Those things were routine by now. I had no idea the danger I was in. I had bought into his worldview as well. Subconsciously, I felt everything was my fault. I didn't know that there is no way to sidestep or engineer the rage of an abuser. In my mind, I just hadn't figured out the formula for peace yet.

I was back home for two weeks when he blew up at me again. It seems crazy that I can't recall exactly what set him off, but by this time Stephen's rages were frequent and usually had a familiar theme. Without realizing it, I had become a master mathematician, always doing the math of how to avoid a blow up. When is the best time to ask a question? Which questions are safe? Is it worth asking for help with this? If something broke, I would make the time to get to a hardware store, find the wood glue, and fix it myself. If I asked for help, Stephen would say, "Can't you do it? I just got home from work." Sometimes I thought back to the day he dropped the dumpster car off at my house. "Can't you just do it?" I remembered his nearly whining. Now I wouldn't press any issue. I did anything to avoid a blow up, but it never worked.

This time I was more strategic. I called my parents and told them I was done and moving home. My parents rented a trailer and grabbed my brother and the three of them drove down. I told them they couldn't come while Stephen was there, that I was too afraid of his causing a scene. They sat at a gas station around the corner, and as soon as he left for work, I called them and they came over. We got all of my stuff packed up and quickly loaded into the trailer. Almost everything was mine. When we were done, he was left with the living room set his parents had purchased for us and his clothes. My heart was racing. Rushing in and out of the apartment to the trailer felt like something from *Mission: Impossible*. We had to get out and be done before he came home. I left a note nailed to the wall directly across from the front door letting him know that I was done.

I rode up to Maine in the car with my dad. The ride was mostly silent. I finally spoke up at one point and asked him if it was normal after seven months of marriage for a husband not to want to have sex with his wife. I can't even imagine what it was like for him to hear or even to have to answer that question. My dad wasn't a talker and he and I definitely never had conversations like this before. He wasn't able to look at me but matter-of-factly said, "No." We finished the rest of our drive in silence. When we got home, I sat at the kitchen counter and cried, and my dad cried with me. I can see his face to this day, crying into a napkin and wiping the tears from his eyes, not speaking between sniffles. I had never seen my father cry before and can't remember ever seeing him cry since.

Later that night I was in bed trying to sleep when my mom came into my room.

"Sarah, Stephen is at the front door. Do you want to talk to him?"

Many of us have that one moment in our lives we would go back and change and our entire world would have been different. This was that moment for me. I should have made a different decision, but I have to believe everything happens for a reason, so I try not to look at this with regret. I said yes. I think the gesture of his driving up to see me caused me to say yes. But now I can't remember for sure. Was I afraid he would make a scene with my parents? Did I say yes to avoid a fight? Whatever it was, I went to the door.

"Can we go for a drive?" he asked.

"Sure," I agreed.

We got in his car and went for a drive and once again this silver-tongued devil convinced me he could change and convinced me to come back. I cried and told him all the things I needed him to change, and he agreed to all of it. He told me all the things that he needed me to do differently, and I agreed to work on and do those things too. Basically, he got me to believe that we were both to blame. I understand now that this is a common tactic of abusers. It's a form of gaslighting. If I did just a few things differently, maybe he wouldn't "have to" get so mad.

His complaints and excuses were all due to work, his being tired from work, and the stress of being the new GM. He said moving to Maine for me and being in a new place was also hard on him. I had wanted to be near my family, so I had obviously ripped him away from his life and family and this caused him stress. This was my fault; he had proof. He was trying to adjust to all these changes. I was in love (or so I thought) and I wanted my marriage to work, so I was relieved to have a reasonable explanation for what was going on. Of course, he was the one who found a transfer to Portland right away. I had to drop out of school and my music program and not return after our wedding. But he did it all for me.

I saw his driving up to Maine as this huge gesture of love. I was like "Gosh, he drove all the way up here in the middle of the night to talk to me—he must really love me." In reality it was just another manipulation tactic. Grand gestures and all that. It was wishful thinking. I wasn't ready to give up on the dream of being a wife and mother. I felt like my leaving may have been the jolt he needed to get in line. I believed that he saw the error of his ways and was really ready to change. Now that I know more about Stephen, I understand his wanting me back was more about preserving his image. Coming home to an empty apartment didn't reflect the persona he wanted to show to the world: happily married, in a fully furnished apartment, with dinner on the stove.

We ended up taking a vacation and flying down to Lake City to visit friends and family. We had an amazing trip. Stephen was relaxed and affectionate; he was the man I married again. We went out for dinners, spent time with his family, and went out with friends. We talked about our future, and we decided that moving to Maine and Massachusetts was a mistake and we should have stayed in Florida. We were so blissfully happy on this vacation I just completely agreed with him. Obviously, he was right all along. I was the selfish one, making him leave everything for me. We had been happy here and we were happy here again. We needed to move back.

Shortly after we got back from our vacation, he got in trouble at work. He told me that he had trusted his assistant manager to send in some new hire paperwork to HR and he failed to do so. Ultimately the blame fell on him as the store manager, so the company was demoting him back to a sales rep. I didn't understand why he was being demoted from management, but he was mad and I didn't want to ask any more questions than I had to. He said he immediately called his old district manager in Florida and asked if he could transfer back down. His old district manager said absolutely; Stephen was one of his top salesmen. In one phone call Stephen was demoted and he was telling me that he could either be a salesman in Massachusetts or we could go back to

Florida. We had only been back from Florida for a few weeks and our conversations and our happy times were still fresh in my mind. It was like this was meant to be. I told him I supported him and we should definitely move back to Florida. This period was the happiest six months of our marriage. He was busy with work, and I was busy packing and working. His aunt Deborah came up to help us finish packing.

On our last day of packing, Deborah and I staged the furniture for moving. As we pulled the couch away from the wall, I saw something large move. Falling away from the wall was a pile, nearly two feet high, of crumpled, crusty, yellowed socks. They had been wedged between the couch and the wall. Stephen was always running out of socks, and he would always just buy more. I could never figure out where they were all disappearing to. Mystery solved. We figured after he came home from work, while I was making dinner, he would sit on the couch, take off his socks and throw them over his shoulder. Who does this? Now I see the towering pile of socks as part of Stephen's magical thinking. It amazes me that he never put two and two together as to where all his socks went. Deborah thought it was the funniest thing she had ever seen and would tell this story many times. Somehow, I never found it quite as amusing as she did.

Six

Grand Slammed at Denny's

In 2008, I got a job working for an insurance company and it paid for me to go back to school for a B.S. in business administration. I was happy and Stephen seemed happy. For a while, anyway.

Once the newness of being back in Florida wore off, he was right back to his old self. We had sunk back into the same routine as before but with the added bonus of some new little games he liked to play. I worked all day, went to class, and then I hurried home to make dinner for him so it would be on the table when he came home. I never knew what mood he would be in or what would set him off. Most evenings it was something trivial like a dish in the sink, the litter box not being freshly scooped, or me working on homework in the living room when he wanted to watch TV. Nearly every night he found some excuse to get mad, and then, let the games begin. My evenings consisted of yelling, name calling, and threats until he stormed off to bed to watch TV or play video games. Dinner would be left to get cold on the table.

A typical night went like this.

I sat down to eat dinner while he stayed in the bedroom until I was almost done only to hear him yell, "I'm hungry!"

At that point I responded, "OK, dinner is still warm. Sit down and have some."

"I don't want anything from you!" was his usual retort.

I finished eating and started to clean up.

He then came out of the bedroom, looked at me with disgust and yelled, "I'm hungry!"

At this point, I was not only upset but also confused. What did he want me to do? I tried to fix it by saying, "I just put the leftovers in the fridge, but I can heat them up in a second."

He looked at me like I was the one acting oddly and said, "I don't want anything from you!" And with that, he stormed back to bed.

Next, I moved to the living room to start on my homework, but was it over? Not even close.

Next thing I knew I heard him yelling, *"I'm hungry!"* At that point I was at the end of my rope, but I still listed every bit of food we had in the house that I could make him for dinner.

He again told me he didn't want anything from me. Then a few minutes later he again yelled about how hungry he was.

This is when I usually gave up on my homework, as I was really at the end of my rope.

Usually, two hours had passed by now. I was exhausted physically and emotionally, and sometimes I burst into tears. I listed all the food in the house again and he would say no to it all again. Then I listed every restaurant in town. Finally, he chose a restaurant from which he found it acceptable for me to buy him food. I called in a take-out order, drove downtown to get it, brought it home and delivered it to him in bed. Once he was satisfied, I had some peace to finish my homework. To this day I don't like to watch TV or snack in bed, as it reminds me of him.

Another cruel little game he liked to play was to scare me. He knew that I was nervous when I was home alone and I wouldn't answer the door unless I knew someone was supposed to be coming. Some days he came home from work early and banged loudly and aggressively on the door. I was, of course, freaked out. When I made my way toward the door to look out the peep hole, my heart racing, it started again: *"Bang bang bang."*

We didn't live in the best part of town and it scared me as it sounded like someone was trying to break the door down. Eventually, he used his key and unlocked the door and laughed hysterically at how he freaked me out. This personality felt like a mixture of Steve-O and The Stephen of Doom. He played it off like he was pulling a prank or practical joke. But it was cruel. He knew how scared I would get and he just loved seeing me upset.

When I went to bed, I often shifted a bit to get comfortable. This bothered Stephen. He got angry with me when I moved in bed. He yelled and sometimes he pushed me. He decided that I was no longer allowed to go to bed until after he had fallen asleep. Of course, he didn't have to go to work as early as I did and he stayed up late every night. Most days I was exhausted. I tried to sleep in the spare room, but that upset him as well. He wanted me to suffer. Once I heard him snoring, I crawled into bed. I had to try really hard not to move too much or else it could wake him. If, in the middle of the night while asleep, I accidentally touched him, he would sit up and punch me and/or kick me hard in the side. Some mornings I woke up with bruises all along my ribs and thighs. The weird thing was I really didn't see this as any sort of domestic violence until a couple years after the divorce. I always used to tell people that he never hit me until the final night I was with him. It feels crazy now that I didn't register that. But I know more about dissociation and how at times I almost left my body to survive.

When going back over my memories, reconstructing my time with Stephen, I found those years after we went back to Florida, from 2008 to 2012, were the years with the biggest holes in my recollections. One memory that came back was when Stephen and I visited my family in February of 2009. We stayed with my parents at their house on China Lake.

One afternoon, Stephen really wanted to go for a snowmobile ride even though it was around 3 o'clock. During the winter in Maine, it gets dark early, around 4. Even though I really didn't want to be out in the wind as the sun was setting, I did what Stephen wanted, and we went out for a ride on the lake. We left the house and headed up the lake, going around the outside of a group of islands. Stephen was going pretty fast, especially for a guy who had never been on a snowmobile before. I was a bit behind him because my shield kept fogging up and I was messing with it, trying to get it clean.

It was starting to get dark, so I caught up to him and suggested we turn around. He agreed. On the way back he again went ahead of me, speeding across the ice. Stephen decided he was going to go between the islands. I followed behind him, and just as he reached the tip of an island, he stopped abruptly. I noticed at the last second and pulled back the throttle to turn but it was too late. I started sliding and hit him sideways. He jumped off right before I hit him and I got my leg pinned between the two snowmobiles. The snowmobiles and I slid across the ice before coming to a stop.

Dazed and in shock at what just happened, I looked back and saw Stephen sitting on the ice looking at me. I struggled to free my leg and get off the sled. Taking a step, I yelled to him, "What happened?! Why did you stop like that?" He didn't say anything; he just looked at me. I took a couple more steps toward the front of my sled and the next thing I knew the ice gave out beneath me. I was in the water.

The hole in the ice was large and I came back up to the surface quickly. I was in full gear with a helmet and all. I screamed, "Stephen, I'm in the water! I'm in the water! I'm in the water!" I heard nothing. I screamed for him again and again. I swam to the edge and tried pulling myself out, but the ice just kept breaking off and I couldn't get out. My gear was saturated and heavy with freezing water now, and I was trying not to panic. But my mind was racing. Where was Stephen? I screamed for him again.

At last, Stephen came over, laid down on the ice and helped pull me out. Once I was out, I rolled and rolled until I thought I was far enough away that the ice supported my weight again. I stood and looked at Stephen. "You should go get help, I'll stay here with the snowmobiles," he said.

It was a long walk to the house from where we had our accident and night was falling quickly. I walked along the shore, stripping off the wet layers of my clothes as I went. I could see other people on their snowmobiles, and I tried to wave at them but my arms felt like they weighed a million pounds. None of them saw me. Shivering, I kept walking. Finally, Stephen came up behind me. He was able to get the snowmobiles out of the water and got one to start. He picked me up and we went back to the house and then he and my dad went out and got the other sled. To this day I have circulation issues in my fingers and toes due to minor frostbite.

After this incident, everyone treated Stephen like a hero because he "saved my life." He responded the first time, "Well, I didn't have life insurance on her yet." People were a little shocked but then started laughing like this was some great joke, albeit a little dark. After that he made this same comment every time the story was told of when I fell through the ice. I went along with the joke and had convinced myself that it was nothing more.

Years later I started to view this scene through a different lens. The accident was not intentional, but I truly believe that the reason he took so long to come to my rescue is because he thought about letting me die. If he had life insurance on me at that time, he never would have saved me.

Towards the end of our marriage, we were in a routine where every night Stephen found something new to be angry about, but things got even worse. Once I was in bed when Stephen's phone went off at about 2:00 a.m. He got out of bed to answer it and then left the apartment to talk outside. He was gone for more than an hour. When he got back, I asked him if everything was OK and he told me it was a work thing. At 2:00 a.m.? By this time, he had worked his way back up to general manager of one of Musician Central's retail locations in Florida so, I suppose he thought that was a believable excuse. I didn't think so.

Six. Grand Slammed at Denny's

I knew better than to press the issue, so I went back to sleep. He started receiving late night phone calls that he took outside around twice a week. Another night, we were in bed, and he thought I was asleep. He had Facebook Messenger open on his phone. I rolled over and he immediately dropped his phone out of my view and looked at me to see if I was awake. My eyes were barely open so he thought they were closed, and as soon as he was comfortable, he picked the phone back up and started chatting again. Through my eyelashes, I snuck a peek at the screen, and it said "Denise." I knew she worked for him at Musician Central. She was also a tattoo model for *Inked* magazine.

I shifted my weight a little and he dropped the phone again. Once he was sure I was asleep, he picked the phone back up. Three more times, I moved ever so slightly, and he reacted the same way each time. I couldn't read what was on the screen, but considering he was hiding his phone, it was something he didn't want his wife to read. I wasn't sure what to do with this information. I knew he was hiding something from me and I knew he was talking to someone. I just didn't have any proof. I was conflicted about how to handle things. If I asked him about it, I knew he would lie and accuse me of being "crazy" and "pathetic." Also, with his volatile temper, there was no way I could confront him. It was already a full-time job for me to keep him from blowing up at me and I really didn't want to "poke the bear," as it were.

I had to figure out if I really cared about this or not. I knew in my heart that I was not in love with this man anymore, so I was angry over the affair but not heartbroken. Would he even miss me if I left? Maybe this was the time to get divorced. I knew I was not happy and obviously he had a new girlfriend, so he might not fight me or come after me. Then my thoughts shifted to all the people who would be affected by my leaving. His parents would be devastated, his aunt would be so upset, my parents would be disappointed in me. I decided to keep quiet for now.

The laptop had a password on it, and every time I asked him for that password, he dodged the question. He started to password protect his phone and wouldn't give me that password either. I was pretty sure he and Denise were having an affair. We had been married almost five years at this point.

The holidays were upon us and Stephen was more difficult than usual. We always spent Christmas Eve with his family opening gifts and having dinner, and on Christmas Day everyone got breakfast together. This year we were to meet at Denny's. Stephen and I were the first people there.

We were there about ten minutes but no one else had arrived.

"Find out where they are," Stephen said. I called his parents.

"Oh, Sarah," his mom said, "I should have called, but we've got an emergency here."

"Emergency? Are you OK?" I looked at Stephen, who could hear the conversation as well.

"Grandpa fell. We're here with Deborah and just making sure he's OK."

"That's awful! Did he call you?"

"Luckily, he was right next to the phone in the hall when he fell. We're just figuring out if he needs to go to the ER."

"OK ... do you want us to come over?"

"Oh, no, stay there, we'll be there soon." She hung up.

"So they're going to be even later?" Stephen looked at me, disgust pouring off of him. There was no worry about his grandfather, only his irritation at being inconvenienced.

"Your mom said they would be here as soon as they can."

"Great. We're just stuck here."

The waitress came by and asked when the rest of our party would be arriving.

"We don't know, OK?" Stephen snapped at her. "Can we get some drinks?"

Our drinks arrived, but his family was nowhere to be seen. As usual, Stephen had spent our accounts dry, so neither of us had money to cover the drinks. The longer we waited, the more he directed his anger at me, as if the situation was entirely my fault. The restaurant was filled with families, grandparents, and kids. Stephen's voice rose over the booths and tables.

"This is fucking rude. Like always, you're not doing a damn thing about it. You're fucking useless. Just useless!"

He obviously had someplace else he would rather be and he didn't want to be kept waiting. The longer we waited, the more he started to tear into me, just being mean and hateful and loud about it. I was so embarrassed.

"Call them." Stephen pointed at my phone. "This is ridiculous. So inconsiderate."

I called them again and they said they were still with Grandpa but leaving in a minute.

"What the fuck? No one ever has any respect for my time!"

"Stephen, it was an emergency ... they didn't do it on purpose."

"You always take their side! Why are you such a bitch? Why can't you take my side just one fucking time?"

I wished I could hide under the table. People were looking at us. The waitress was talking to someone who looked like a manager, both of them giving us sidelong glances. I knew there was no way to calm him down now. He was full of self-righteous anger and ready to go after anyone who said anything at all to him.

"Whatever. I can't wait here all day for these people." He grabbed the car keys and strode out of the restaurant. There I was at Denny's, alone, no money, no car, no idea when his family would be there, and I was just cussed out in front of the entire restaurant, on Christmas morning, no less. Merry Christmas.

Finally, Roger, Carol, and Deborah showed up and I immediately started to cry. Through tears and hyperventilation, I explained to them what happened. None of them were even phased by it. Years later, I wondered if they were so blasé because they had seen this behavior from Stephen his entire life. For me, even after five years of marriage, it was still shocking. His berating me in public. The oversized tantrums, not caring who heard or saw him behaving that way. But for them, it seemed normal, an everyday occurrence. We had breakfast and I went home with Deborah. I ended up staying with her for a few days because I didn't want to go home, and Stephen wouldn't come get me. Finally, Deborah took me back home.

A few days later, Stephen came home from work in a great mood. This was very unusual. I should have known something was up. I made spaghetti for dinner, and it was sitting on the table ready to eat when he got there. He strolled in and grabbed a drink.

"You remember my friend Carl?" he asked.

"I'm not sure. Is he at Musician Central?"

"Nah. He was an old friend from before I started working there. He moved to Texas. Anyway, I was talking to him today and he and his wife got divorced."

I nodded and thought to myself, "OK, where are you going with this, Stephen?"

"They still love each other and everything, they're still friends, but they just couldn't be married. It's been a real positive experience for them." He paused and looked at me. "I was thinking maybe we could do that."

"Do what? Get divorced?" My voice squeaked a little on the word "divorce."

"Yeah. You know, our lives are kind of headed in different directions. I mean, you're on your path and I'm on mine ... why stay married?"

He had never mentioned divorce before, not even during his worst blow-ups. My head was spinning. We discussed every aspect of the whole scene. We determined how all of our stuff would get split up. He kept repeating that our lives were leading us to different places. At the time, I didn't really see this. It was clear we were headed in very different directions, but that certainly wasn't the source of misery in our marriage. He talked more about us being friends after the divorce, and about how since we only had three months left on our lease and there were two bedrooms, I could just move into the spare room until the lease was up. Then we could each find our own places.

Then he had the most absurd idea ever. He said we should get divorced and not tell anyone. He wanted to wait until the divorce was final and then throw a party. At the party, with everyone gathered, we would say, "Surprise! We're divorced!"

As this bizarre conversation went on, my mind was in two places. On the one hand, I was relieved. I had an out. I could move into the spare room, no more bruises, no more interrupted sleep. The divorce was Stephen's idea, so he wouldn't come after me or blow up in some unexpected way. It sounded too good to be true. On the other hand, I was devastated. I kept thinking of our disappointed families, my sense of failure, divorced at twenty-six; it was overwhelming. What made it worse was his over-the-top cheerful attitude. He was reminding me of a three-ring circus ringmaster, "Ladies and gentlemen! Step right up for a fabulous, stupendous, remarkable divorce!" I found myself crying while he went on about the benefits of our impending divorce.

Then, all of a sudden, he stopped and said, "Let's not decide now. Let's think about it." I cleaned up dinner and he went to bed.

A couple days went by, and I was still reeling. I thought of nothing else. The more I thought about it, the more the positives outweighed the negatives. I kept thinking of how he removed the fear of leaving for me. He gave me permission to divorce him! I'm free! I decided to make my move. He came home from work one night and seemed to be in a decent mood, so I decided this was a good time. He grabbed a soda from the fridge, and I asked, "Have you given any more thought to our conversation from the other night?"

"No, I haven't."

"Well, I have, and I think you're right. We should get divorced."

He looked at me, said, "OK," and walked into the bedroom.

Six. Grand Slammed at Denny's

I couldn't believe it was so easy. I walked into the bedroom and told him that I would sleep in the spare bedroom for now as we previously discussed. I grabbed my pillow and some blankets. He was happy with the arrangement. The biggest issue for him was his family. He didn't want to tell them yet and made me promise not to say anything. We agreed that when the time came, we would go together, sit his parents down, and tell them. They would realize that we were both OK and hopefully it would soften the blow.

For Stephen it was about his image. He didn't want anything to mar his façade. I slowly started sorting through closets and packing my things for an eventual move.

On January 3, 2012, our sixth wedding anniversary, I was in the spare room sleeping when Stephen came home late. He had been out drinking with some guys after work. He walked into my room with a bag of string cheese.

"Happy anniversary!" He swayed a bit, and his words were slurred.

"Happy anniversary, Stephen. Good night," I said, half-asleep.

He pulled out a piece of the string cheese. "I got you something. Here's your anniversary present!"

"Thanks, but I'm not hungry and I don't want it right now."

Before I could register what was happening, he leaned over the bed and slapped me in the face with the bag of cheese.

"You're an ungrateful bitch, you know that?"

I sat up. "Leave me alone. I just want to sleep."

He pushed me against the wall, hard. I could feel my back and then my head hit the wall, like whiplash.

He shook his head at me, looked at me with disgust and left the room. I didn't move, listening hard for what he was doing. In a few minutes he was back in the doorway.

"You always ruin everything, don't you? I do everything for you, and you can't be nice for even a minute. You're always such a bitch."

I was still disoriented from sleep and from being thrown against the wall. Where could I go? How could I get this to stop? He blocked the doorway so I couldn't leave. The spare room wasn't so much a bedroom as a storage room with a bed in it. Over the last few days, between school and work, I hadn't the time to make it more livable. He stepped into the room and kicked a box of books on the floor.

"You're disgusting. This room is disgusting. Lazy, disgusting, ungrateful loser." He pulled a book out of the box. What was he doing? He threw it at my head. I dodged it but was afraid to hide. Hiding might make him angrier. He pulled out another book and threw it. Shoes, a glass bowl (a wedding gift), a lamp; he was grabbing whatever was near and hurling it at me. I curled up against the wall and put my arms over my head. I was afraid to look but afraid not to.

He left the room, crashed around the living room, and came back. He threw something else. I don't even remember what it was. I was paralyzed. He left again and came back, this time leaning over me and yelling so forcefully I could feel his spit landing on my arms. Finally, he left again and didn't come back for a while. My ears strained to hear where he might be or what he was doing. After what felt like an hour, I crept to the door and heard him snoring in his room. This was the first time he had really laid hands on me that I was aware of. I made the decision right then that I couldn't stay there a minute longer. I packed up a few things and snuck out.

That was the last time I saw him.

SEVEN

"How am I supposed to eat?"

"Holy crap, what did I just do?"

I sat in my car absorbing that I just left my home in the middle of the night. I moved the seat all the way back to give myself space to breathe. It was dark outside except for the glow of the streetlights in the parking lot.

My mind reeled. Should I go back? No. I never wanted to see him again. I was exhausted but also full of adrenaline. I started to feel scared. What was he going to do when he woke up and found I wasn't there? Would he come after me?

I didn't have a place to go. It was 2:00 a.m., so I drove to work on auto pilot. When the sun came up, I went inside. There were showers in the onsite gym, so I took a long shower to wash off the night and then went upstairs to work. I tried to focus on what I had to get done that day but it was impossible. As I sat at my desk, I could feel the tears slowly falling down my cheeks. I tried to keep my head down as much as possible, so no one would see that I was falling apart.

I spent most of the day texting with my cousin. It was a time for strategy and action. We talked about what my next steps were. I needed to find a place to live. A quick search on Apartments.com brought up dozens of options.

I needed to figure out how much I could afford in rent. I worked up a budget sheet. I had about $400–$500 for rent and utilities. I narrowed my search to those price ranges, looking for places that included utilities in the rent. I found four places that could work. I called each place to schedule times to see the apartments.

That second night I stayed in the parking lot again. The next morning, as I waited for the elevators, one of my friends from work walked up to me.

She smiled at me like any other day. "Hey, good morning! How are things?"

I looked at her and immediately started crying. She grabbed me into a hug and pulled me into the corner so I would have some privacy.

"What's wrong?" She was obviously concerned.

"I left my husband the other night," I blurted out.

She hugged me again. "Oh, Sarah, I'm so sorry, but you'll be fine. Tons of people are divorced. It's not the end of the world."

Her words didn't matter or really even register. It was just nice to say it out loud, and it was nice to have someone hug me. I knew I couldn't share the truth with her. What if I had said, "Divorce may be normal, but my husband is dangerous and I'm so afraid, I'm living in the parking lot"?

Today was the first day of training for a promotion I had just received. I got to my assigned seat and thought to myself, "I haven't heard from Stephen." I was surprised that he hadn't called or texted me. I wasn't sure if this was a good thing or a bad thing, like the calm before the storm. I brushed the thought quickly out of my head and focused on the training. I needed this promotion more than ever, as I would be on my own from now on.

On my lunch break I looked at apartments. I found one in the same apartment complex that a co-worker lived in. Caroline and I had recently become friends when I was supervising a project that she was on. The complex was enormous with dozens of brick buildings enveloped by mature oak trees dripping with Spanish moss. It was a cute little one-bedroom, one-bath apartment on the second floor. Rent was $465 and included all utilities and basic cable; I could do this! I went to the office, filled out the application and went back to work. The next day I got the call that the apartment was mine and I could move in whenever I was ready. My relief was immediate and profound. I had a place to live, I had money, I had a plan. I was going to be OK.

I went to the bank to get the money to pay the first and last months' rent and the security deposit. When the teller pulled up my account she blushed and looked awkwardly at me.

"Mrs. Jones, your account has been overdrawn. You have a negative balance of $248.00."

I felt my face heating up and knew I was turning a dark shade of crimson.

"I can tell by your face that this is a surprise to you."

"Where did the money go?" I was dumbfounded and embarrassed.

She printed out a log of recent transactions and we reviewed it together. Stephen and I had a joint account with debit cards. Over a period of three days, there were charges at Best Buy, Foot Locker, Sharper Image, four restaurants, and a handful of other stores. It looked as if he had gone on a shopping tour of the local mall. I was in shock. Sitting there in the bank, I felt like crying again, but I was almost out of tears and definitely getting bored with crying in public. What could I tell the apartment complex manager?

I decided I needed to be completely honest. I told the lady in the office that I had left my husband and he had spent all our money over the last week.

"I'll get paid in two weeks and I'll have the money then if you can hold it." I held my breath.

"Honey, I can hold it for you. It sounds like you're going through it." She had a sympathetic voice. "But if you don't have it in two weeks, I'm sorry, but I'll have to give it to the next person in line."

"Thank you so much." I felt like crying again. Would this ever stop? My relief and gratitude felt overwhelming. I told someone the truth and the world didn't end and I still had the apartment.

I spent the following two weeks living in my Honda Civic. I knew security wouldn't be thrilled with my new living arrangements, so I took precautions. After work I drove around until it was dark. Sometimes I went to the university library or walked around the campus to kill time. I didn't have any close friends. Friendships had been difficult while living with Stephen.

After 10 o'clock, when security for the building was lighter, I drove into the back of the west parking lot and settled in for the night. My clothes were all in the backseat. I pulled out what I planned on wearing the next day and laid it over the rest of my clothes to get the wrinkles out. Sleeping in a car is uncomfortable; the slightest noise wakes you up, there is no room to roll over and sleeping on your back feels so vulnerable. Luckily, I thought to bring a pillow and a blanket when I left, so at least I had those. If you're tired enough you'll sleep anywhere. I wasn't afraid since the south side of Lake City was a land of mansions and gated communities. Sleeping in a car at night was safer than where I had been.

At six every morning, I drove around to the east parking lot, waved at the security guards, and headed to the shower in the gym. I was grateful that the cafeteria served breakfast, lunch, and dinner and prices were deeply discounted for employees. My cousin wired me money for food. Oatmeal in the morning was about $2.00. Coffee was $1.50 if I brought my own cup. For lunch there was always a $5.00 special. Dinner always

59

had cheap options using leftovers from the lunch menu so I could get dinner for around $8.00. I was able to live on about $18.00 a day.

On day five of my being gone, Stephen sent me a text. "So do you plan on coming home at some point?"

Ugh. I really didn't want to talk to him. I replied with a simple "No."

I was both surprised that he texted and not surprised. Divorce was his idea, and he wanted me gone, but only on his timetable. That I had left in the middle of the night, due to his unstable and dangerous behavior, was not in keeping with his plan. He liked to be in control.

After what felt like the longest two weeks of my life it was finally payday. I was waiting for my lunch break to go to the bank when my phone rang. It was the bank.

"Good morning, Sarah, could you please come down to the bank as soon as you can?"

"Sure, I'll be right down." I had no clue what it could calling about.

At the bank, I asked the teller what was going on.

"Your account is overdrawn by $300."

"I don't understand. My paycheck just deposited this morning."

She pulled up my account and, once again, we went through the charges together. Stephen had been on another shopping spree. There was a $300 charge at the Apple store, $200 at Lucky Brand jeans, and a large cash withdrawal. The Apple charge was the last to clear that very morning, and the one that took the account into the negative. This was too much. I couldn't help myself and burst into tears. Blowing my nose and drying my eyes, I explained what was going on in my life. We made a plan. I cancelled my direct deposit so that my next paycheck would come to me as a paper check. I told her I didn't have the money to bring the account current, but that Stephen's paycheck would be going into the account next Friday.

At this point I threw in the proverbial towel. I knew I couldn't do this on my own. I got back to my desk, picked up the phone and called my mom.

"Mom, I left Stephen. I don't have a place to live, but I found an apartment. Stephen cleaned out the bank accounts and I'm going to lose this apartment if I can't provide the first and last months' rent and security deposit today. Can you and Dad help me?"

In true motherly fashion, without skipping a beat or asking any questions, she answered, "Who do I call and will they take a credit card over the phone?"

That afternoon, I slept on an air mattress in my new apartment. My mom and I reached out to my aunt and she bought me some furniture and a bed to get me started. Over the next two weeks I snuck back over to the apartment where Stephen still lived and filled up my car with as much of my stuff as I could and brought it to my new apartment.

The next pay day, I got my paper check and opened a new bank account at a different bank. I felt happy and relieved that my money was now my own as I got into my car. My phone rang. I looked at the screen and the caller ID showed that it was Stephen. I thought about not answering for a minute, but this was the first time he had reached out on the phone since I left more than two weeks ago, so I answered. Before I could even say "Hello," he started in.

"There's no money in the bank account!"

"Yes, I know. You spent it all."

"No, you got paid today. There should be money in the account!"

"I opened up my own bank account, Stephen. We are no longer together. I now have my paychecks going into my own bank account."

"Well, how am I supposed to eat?" He was screaming at me by this point.

I paused and took a breath. "I don't know. Maybe you should return the $200 worth of jeans you bought at Lucky or the $300 worth of stuff you bought at Apple. You weren't worried about how I was going to eat when you over-drafted our accounts then. And frankly, how you eat is no longer any of my concern." I felt oddly calm in that moment.

As soon as I hung up, my heart started racing, but I had done it. I stood up for myself and told him just how I felt. That felt really good, but I was also more thankful than ever that I worked in a building with armed security guards. Even now that I wasn't with him, telling him the truth felt risky.

Even though I was relieved to be on my own, I was still confused about why my marriage didn't work. I was convinced I had done something wrong. I lived in an area where you didn't get divorced. If you did, it was frowned upon by the church and everyone went to church. Prayer and counsel by a pastor should have been enough to fix my marriage, so why didn't that work for me? Well, aside from the fact that my husband wouldn't go to counseling or church.

Over the course of my marriage, I felt the support of church was taken from me too. Stephen grew up going to his family's church, so everyone there knew him from childhood. I was an outsider and didn't feel comfortable talking to the pastor, as I worried it would embarrass his family. When we moved back to Florida, I was asked to join the worship team. I was excited about this, as it meant I would sing more often instead of just singing with my father-in-law on special occasions. Suddenly, Stephen didn't want me going to church. I could only go to church on the days Stephen worked or on the rare occasion he wanted to go. He made it seem like he wanted to spend time with me on Sunday, as he worked every other day of the week. I thought that was sweet, so I was OK with it at the time. I see now that this was another isolation tactic and another way to control me.

When we went to church, it felt like he was only going to show off to his friends who were still regular members. He walked in with an air of arrogance. His "Stephen" personality was on display, looking around, scanning the pews, making sure everyone knew he was there. I just wanted to get into church, sit down, pray, listen to the message, and leave when it was over. Church for me was not about being the best dressed or the most successful, but Stephen wanted the people in his church to know he was superior and busy with his career, and that's why he couldn't come more often. I missed having a community through church. Over my entire life I always made friends through church. It was my whole life.

Without the familiar support of the church, I felt completely alone. A month had gone by since I left Stephen and I was just trying to handle everything on my own. My cousin Kathy was in D.C. at the time and I talked to her on the phone, but she was the only person I felt comfortable talking with in any detail about my ordeal. From other people, I felt a lot of judgment, but I didn't feel ready to tell anyone what I had been through.

There were a few people who saw through Stephen. Those people made comments about how they couldn't believe I was married to him or they complained to me about the things he did that upset them, like it was my fault or maybe there was something I could do about it. At every turn, I couldn't win and felt overwhelmingly like a failure.

Years later, when I gradually started telling people in my circle about the realities of my marriage, there was a persistent recurring theme. People found it shocking that abuse could happen to a woman who is educated and career-focused with a loving family and good friends, as if any of those things is a good luck charm against domestic abuse. Most of them would say what maybe all of them were thinking: "I can't believe this happened to you—I thought you were stronger than that."

Seven. *"How am I supposed to eat?"*

There is an enduring and ridiculous idea that if someone is abused, they weren't strong enough to stop it or smart enough to see it coming. There are people out there that hit you like the bus you never saw barreling down the street. By the time you realize the bus is there, it's too late and you've been run over. Some of us are lucky enough to survive the blow. If you think it takes anything less than incredible strength to withstand the hit, then I promise you, you are wrong.

During the months after leaving, I did everything I could not to be alone with my thoughts. However, at night there were no distractions and in sleep the nightmares would come. One vivid dream always started with me in my apartment, sleeping in my bed. A dark figure came in through the front door, walked through the apartment and into my bedroom. The figure sat down on the bed and leaned over me. In the dream I could feel the weight of his body sitting on the side of the mattress. I could hear his breathing and prayed he would go away if I just kept my eyes shut. But I always opened my eyes. The moonlight shone through the window and illuminated my husband's face, staring at me in the dark with no expression. I get goosebumps just writing about this dream even now. It would wake me out of a deep sleep every time I had it.

I began to make friends at work. But I was still devastatingly lonely and confused. I hit a level of hopelessness where I had to get help or end my life, and I opted to get help.

One day Caroline gave me a little book, *What the Bible Says About Divorce*. I avoided reading it. Growing up in the church, I knew that divorce was a terrible sin. I was already feeling bad; I didn't need to feel worse. Finally, one night the sadness was overwhelming, and I had the nightmare again, so with no other ideas I picked up the book. The first thing I read was "Your builders will be faster than your destroyers." As I looked closer at the book, I saw it was all about the emotions that a person feels while going through a divorce. For each emotion the book gave scriptures or words of comfort related to the Bible.

Being slightly Type A (OK, maybe more than slightly), I immediately started a pro/con– style list of my Builders and my Destroyers. My Builders list very quickly quadrupled the size of my Destroyers list. Feeling a little bit of hope, I remembered my employer had recently handed out information on the employee assistance program. I grabbed the brochure and called the hotline number to get connected with a counselor in my area. There was some relief in taking this step. But I still felt like such a failure, like there was some mystical thing I was missing. I knew I couldn't figure it out on my own, so there I was, driving to a therapist's office.

That day was just like a lot of days in Central Florida. The sun was shining, and the outside of the building was meticulously landscaped with tall palm trees swaying slightly in the breeze. I never got used to Florida landscaping. In Maine trees are allowed to be trees and shrubs are scattered about wherever they choose to be. In Florida, I noticed developers cut everything down and started with an alien, flat surface. The resulting fresh landscaping always looked as if it were done by someone who could barely recall what the natural world looked like.

The entrance to her office felt hidden around the side of the building. As I walked around the building, I remember wondering if the entrance was hidden because people didn't want to be seen going to therapy. I opened the door and was greeted by a small, comfortable lobby with two armchairs, two small tables, a lamp, and some magazines. It could have been a relative's living room. There were two doors and each one had a sign: "In Session." There was a soundtrack of some soothing sounds playing. It reminded me of what a spa might be like. I took a seat and waited for one of the doors to open. I still had time to back out, to get up and leave.

I didn't know what to expect. I'm from Maine, not New York City. I had never spoken to a therapist before. At that time where I was from, there was still a bit of stigma behind it. Like, if you talk to a therapist, you're crazy, right? Well, if I'm being honest, I sure felt a little crazy back then. I was also living in Central Florida, in the Bible Belt. Going to church should have made all my problems disappear.

I know it was less than five minutes, but after what felt like hours, a nice-looking older woman opened the door. Her client said goodbye, smiled and left. I wasn't even sure of the etiquette for this exchange. Should I be averting my gaze in case her client didn't want to be recognized? I was a fish out of water, completely unsure of the territory.

She introduced herself. "Are you Sarah?"

I quietly confirmed that I was, and she invited me into her office. It was like a big living room. Very comfy and not clinical at all. I don't know if I was expecting an actual doctor's office complete with an exam table covered with white paper. It wasn't like the movies or a magazine cartoon either. No chaise to lie on and be examined like Freud. She invited me to take a seat on a well-worn red leather couch and asked, "What are we here for today?"

Oh God, where do I even start? I told her that over Christmas break I left my husband, and I was struggling with depression related to that.

"I just can't understand what went wrong, why he was so mean to me, why didn't he love me. I don't understand what I did to deserve this." The words just poured out of me like a volcano erupting from this massive build-up of pressure just below the surface. Now the tears were falling freely, and all of my emotions were bubbling up. She reached over and grabbed a box of tissues and passed them to me.

"Tell me about what happened. Why do you feel like he didn't love you?"

I told her about the yelling, the name calling, the games, his cruelty, and the last night with the cheese "anniversary gift."

She was quiet for a moment and then she said, "The behaviors you are describing are domestic abuse and violence. I don't think the question is what you did to deserve the actions. I think no matter what you did, he would have behaved this way."

It was like the floor dropped out from beneath me and I found my footing all at the same time. I thought I knew what domestic violence was. I was telling myself, "He really only hit me the one time when he was slapping me in the face with the bag of cheese, and then when he shook me and banged me against the wall." The rest I thought was ... well, I didn't know what it was. I thought I wasn't as lucky as the other couples I knew who didn't fight like that, or maybe they did fight like that because he usually did it behind closed doors. Once I had a name for my experience, I felt like a weight had been lifted off of me. I felt like a sick person with no idea of why they are sick getting test after test, until finally one day the doctor says you have *this*! Suddenly my problem had a name and I had something I could fight. It gave me permission to no longer blame myself. I didn't fail at the marriage.

I was dodging calls from my in-laws. I couldn't lie to them. I still respected Stephen's wishes not to tell them about the divorce, so I opted to avoid them. After a few weeks, his Aunt Deborah left me a voicemail telling me she knew something was wrong and I needed to call her back immediately. Deborah and I were very close, friends, really. We hung out, I was often at her house, and we regularly had dinner and drinks, just the two of us. She was honestly my only friend as Stephen had driven away the rest of them.

I knew I needed to tell her, so I called her back. She was with a family friend, Mary Jean, when I called, so I invited both of them to my new place. The three of us sat there in my barely furnished apartment while I shared with them some of the stories of why I was not happy with Stephen. We talked and cried together.

Mary Jane looked at me and Deborah and said out loud what I believe Deborah needed to hear from a third party. "What he did to you, that's abuse."

Eight

"What did Stephen tell you?"

Deborah looked at Mary Jane and I looked at Deborah. Since that day with my therapist, I was just getting used to the term "abuse" myself. But I was so relieved that Mary Jane said it out loud now, in front of Deborah, because I never could have told her on my own. This was her nephew; I never wanted to say anything bad about him to her or to his parents, for that matter. Deborah said she wished that I hadn't waited so long to tell her that Stephen and I were separated. But she understood that it was Stephen's decision and I wanted to respect it. She agreed not to tell Carol and Roger but to let Stephen and I do it together. The next night I got a call from Deborah at around 9:30.

"Sarah, Stephen just left here. He showed up unannounced and told me about the divorce. Now, he's heading over to his parents' house."

It's like he had a sixth sense or something. I just told Deborah last night. Now he was at her house the next day? Maybe she told him she knew? She said she wouldn't. I was so confused. Why was he doing this without me? This was not what we agreed to. It was so important to him to keep up appearances, to make sure his family knew he didn't do anything wrong. I was doing what he asked by not telling them. Why was he ruining his own plan now?

I sat alone in my apartment trying to focus on the paper I was writing for my complex decision-making class. Around 10 o'clock my phone lit up and started ringing. I saw my in-laws' home number flashing across the screen.

I took a deep breath and answered it, mustering up the happiest voice I could. "Hi!"

"Hello, Sarah, where are you?" It was Roger. I could hear a small sniffle.

"I'm at home," I answered, my voice a little less enthusiastic.

"Stephen just left here. Can you come over?" It seemed as if he was trying to hide the fact that he was crying. My heart was breaking as I heard this in his voice.

"Yes, I'll be right over," I told him. I could hear Carol crying in the background as well.

"OK, thanks. See you soon," he replied, and then we hung up.

I was in my pajamas, so I changed into some clothes and drove to their house. When I arrived, I headed in through the garage. I knocked lightly and let myself in as usual.

I saw Roger in the kitchen making Carol some tea. He turned to look at me, and his face was red with tears. He pointed to the family room at the back of the house and said, "Mom needs you."

I walked around the corner and saw Carol sitting in the dimly-lit room on the couch hugging a pillow and crying. She looked up at me unable to speak through her tears. I took a seat next to her and hugged her for a while, rubbing her back to try and soothe her. I quietly assured her that I was OK. Roger made his way in and placed a cup of tea on the table for her.

At this point I was very aware that they knew about the divorce, though we hadn't yet said it out loud. I was overwhelmed by the emotional destruction I walked into. We sat quietly for what seemed like an eternity but in reality was only a few seconds. What did he say to them? We had talked about how we would make this experience as positive as possible for them. I knew they would be sad, but what I was seeing here was desolation.

I broke the silence first. "So, what did Stephen tell you?"

Roger answered, "He came over unannounced. He didn't come in all the way. He just stood in the kitchen doorway and told us he couldn't stay, but he wanted to let tell us that the two of you are getting divorced. He said he didn't come here to discuss it or to answer any questions about it. He was just letting us know it's happening. Before we could even speak, he turned around and left."

What a monster. Who does that to their parents? This was such a cold and unfeeling way to break news like this to someone. My in-laws and I were extremely close. I spent more time with them than their son. He knew this would devastate them; he simply didn't care.

Roger continued. "We knew we wouldn't get anything out of Stephen, so that's when I called you. You got here faster than I expected." He looked puzzled. It was time to come clean.

I was still sitting next to Carol, comforting her and rubbing her back to assure her that things were OK. "Well, I moved out over a month ago," I started.

Eight. "What did Stephen tell you?"

They both looked down at the floor. "I have an apartment in Oak Terrace right around the corner from you, actually." At this news they perked up a little and started to look at me.

Carol mustered up a question amidst the sobs. "Why? What happened? You're like our daughter and now we will never see you again!"

I paused before answering. I was desperate to tell them the truth. That their son is a monster. He is mean and cruel. He is awful to me. I couldn't take it anymore.

I quickly decided that I couldn't do that to them. They were both devastated, and this was their child. I was the one who would be gone in the end. Did I want to taint their opinions of their son? Did I need to unburden myself at their expense? I loved these people. I was closer to them than most of my own family. I couldn't hurt them. It hurt me to see them hurt. I felt their pain so much that I would be willing to ignore my own pain and suffering to make theirs go away.

I decided to tell them what they needed to hear. But they also needed to understand that things would not be fixed. I was done. "Stephen and I are just moving in different directions. We want different things out of life; he wants to keep moving farther down south and my life is here in Lake City. My job and school keep me here."

I was throwing everything I could think of at them. Hollow excuses that I could see they weren't buying. Their faces said, "These were not the reasons a woman leaves her husband."

I decided to switch my strategy. "Stephen isn't happy with me. He's aggravated and mad all the time. You saw him at Christmas; he was mean and angry. I don't make him happy and at this point he is making my life miserable." They exchanged glances and it began to feel like they were starting to understand, but what they understood I am not sure. They knew how mean and manipulative their son could be; it felt like they were starting to read between the lines of what I was saying.

I continued, "Stephen and I talked this out and we are both OK with the decision."

They just looked at each other and remained silent. I think they knew I was holding back and decided they didn't want to know any more. Their questions about the "why" of things stopped.

Carol started to cry again and between sniffles she said, "We are never going to see you again! Please, don't leave us. We love you. You're the daughter I never had. Promise that you will stay in contact with us."

I grabbed her and pulled her in for a hug. "I'm not divorcing you. I am divorcing your son," I blurted out before I could really think about what that meant. While we continued hugging, both of us crying, I suddenly thought how I didn't want Stephen to know where I was. He was still very angry with me, and when he was in a rage, he was unpredictable and scary. When he drank, it was worse.

I looked at Roger and Carol. "I will stay in your life. I love you both and want to continue a relationship with you. But I've moved out. I tried to get my things from the apartment, and I set up my own bank accounts. Stephen is having a hard time accepting this. He is being very..." I paused. I wanted to say "cruel" but I felt I couldn't say that to them. "...mean and I do not want him to know where I live. If we have a relationship, it needs to be separate from Stephen. You cannot tell him where I live." They both agreed to these terms.

It was getting late. I asked them to dinner at my new apartment and again assured them that I was divorcing their son and not them. As I gave them the address my breath caught for a moment. I realized Stephen now had a direct connection to me if his parents turned out not to be who I believed they were. I went home feeling physically and emotionally drained. I tried to catch a few hours of sleep before I had to get up for work. At the time, I wasn't even thinking of how, when talking to Stephen's parents, I had naturally taken the blame for the divorce. It was my automatic role now, to take the blame for everything. Without even thinking of it, I was always covering for him. I drifted off slowly, trying to clear my mind, but as sleep finally found me, so did the nightmares.

I met with an attorney for an initial consultation on filing for divorce. I let him know that I was afraid of Stephen, how he was reasonable for a couple days but then would erupt with rage over the smallest things. The lawyer assured me that he could get this all done. It would be easy as we didn't have children or own any property together. Then he advised that he required a $4,000 retainer. The glimmer of hope he had just given me was gone in a puff of smoke.

"I barely have money to eat at this point. There is no way I can afford $4,000," I explained.

"Well, I would be happy to take your case once you do." I got up and left his office feeling defeated.

I started doing research on how to file for divorce in Florida. I found that I was able to print the divorce papers myself off their website. From there I went down to the county clerk's office, filed the paperwork and got the papers to deliver to the sheriff's office in the county where he lived and worked to have him served. I drove to the sheriff's office in his county and gave them the divorce papers, a photo of him, his work address, and paid them to have him served. Once served he was given 30 days to sign or contest the divorce. He never signed the papers or contested the divorce. I went back to the county clerk's office and asked to file a motion for default which is when you request a court date to finalize the divorce after your spouse fails to meet their obligation or defaults on their 30 days to respond.

I was grateful for my therapist during this process. As I was already in a fragile state of mind, every step of filing for divorce was a mental health crisis for me. After I talked to the lawyer I was in panic mode. "Oh! A $4,000 retainer is all you need? So, Mr. Attorney, did you miss the part where I told you Stephen cleaned out my bank accounts and ruined my credit and I am flat broke?" I had to call my therapist to talk me down.

I was relieved to find the documents online, but they still required so much information. As I filled out each page, I became more overwhelmed. Our marriage was reduced to numbers, accounts, balances, assets, or lack thereof. Questions of who gets the TV in the bedroom vs. the TV in the living room. Every time I had to contact him to answer these questions was like falling into chaos once again. Each text exchange and his venomous replies reminded me how lucky I was to have a therapist for a reality check.

"Stephen, can I have the TV from the bedroom? It's the smaller TV so you can have the big one."

"What about the bikes? I want both bikes! You're too fat to ride yours anyway and I can at least sell it and get the money back for it."

"OK, I don't care about the bike. I am asking about the TVs. Which one can I have?"

"Well, we bought the one in the bedroom with my bonus money from a couple years ago so I'm keeping that one and I really need the big one for my video games."

Without my therapist I would have felt like I was falling into a well of Stephen's crazy. She calmly walked me through it, peeled back the confusion, and reminded me his behavior wasn't normal.

"What do you want to do?" she asks.

"I need a TV. I don't have one right now."

"OK, is the TV worth what he is putting you through to get it?"

"No, but everyone keeps telling me I need to fight him and get all these things."

"Is that what you want to do? Do you want to fight him?"

"No. The only thing I want from him is my freedom."

"Well, then, focus on that. Only fight for what is worth having not just for the sake of fighting or making a point. You need to do what is best for your mental health and if letting him have the stuff and not engaging in the fight does that then I don't see anything wrong with that."

This concept was a life saver. From that point on I didn't ask him for what I wanted. I just put it in the divorce papers and he could contest it or not. I wasn't giving him any more of my energy.

Between filing the divorce paperwork, paying to have Stephen served, and filing a motion for default, it cost me just over $400 to get before a judge for the divorce.

Finally, on September 18, 2012, I waited outside the courtroom for my name to be called. One would think that at this moment I would be happy and excited that it would all be over soon. This was not the case; it was one of the longest 30 minutes of my life waiting in that lobby. I sat among fifteen other people waiting their turn for the judge to hear their cases, but I felt completely alone.

I also felt afraid. Stephen still had one more chance to show up and contest the divorce even though he ignored the paperwork he received and a summons to appear at court for the divorce proceedings. At this point he could show up and tell the judge that he didn't want the divorce or that he didn't agree with what I asked for. I was terrified and had visions of his twisted, angry face appearing from the elevator. He was so much better at talking than I was and was so charismatic that I believed he would show up and convince the judge of anything. I found myself holding my breath every time the elevator door opened, praying it wasn't going to be him stepping off. At last, the doors to the courtroom opened and my name and Stephen's were called. I was ushered into the court and in front of the judge alone. I still had a twinge at the back of my neck that Stephen would walk in at the last minute behind me.

The courtroom was not what I expected. It didn't look like a courtroom from one of those dramas on TV. The walls were dark and the chairs where the public could sit were cast in shadow. I stood beside what looked like a folding table with a faux wood top. The bailiff stood behind me at the door. The judge walked in from a side entrance and took a seat behind a divider, which seemed to have an elevated floor. The judge was so high above me I had to tilt my head to look up at him.

The judge looked down to see who he was presiding over; his eyes scanned the dimly lit courtroom.

"Where is your husband?" he asked.

Eight. *"What did Stephen tell you?"*

"I honestly don't know, Your Honor," I replied, thinking, "Is that right? Do I call him 'Your Honor'?" I had never been in court in my life and the only things I knew came from watching too many episodes of *Law & Order*. I was so nervous my hands and knees were shaking.

He looked down at the paperwork in front of him. I assumed those were my divorce papers. I felt like it was taking a long time for him to review them. I didn't know what normally happened in a divorce proceeding and I had no lawyer to advise or reassure me. Could the judge deny my divorce if I messed up the paperwork? Would I have my life and my freedom today? My fate was in the hands of this human, this man, this judge. I started to feel lightheaded as the thoughts circling my mind seemed to make the room spin with them.

Finally, the judge looked up and said with a tone of annoyed indifference, "Since Mr. Jones doesn't seem to care enough to be here, I am going to grant you everything you are asking for."

"Thank you," I replied with a big gush of air leaving my body. I didn't even realize I had been holding my breath. I felt like crying and took a deep breath in as the ground started to feel more stable beneath me.

The judge's voice took a softer tone as he addressed me while looking me directly in the eye. "Let me advise you. Based on what I am reading and the fact that Mr. Jones hasn't responded to the papers or shown up here today, unless out of the goodness of his heart he pays you what he owes and what I am granting in this divorce, you will have to sue him for it. These papers tell him what you are owed, but they don't compel him to comply."

Again, all I said was "Thank you." What he said hadn't fully sunk in yet.

"I also see that you would like to go back to your maiden name, so that is granted as well."

And with that I was officially divorced.

NINE

"Just tell me
what you want"

Once you've been through domestic abuse, you are now a member of a club that no one wants to join.

You can't relate to people in normal relationships, and they can't relate to you. You might feel lonely even when surrounded by friends and family. It's impossible to explain your thoughts and feelings in a way that makes sense to people who aren't in the club. When they get into an argument with their partner, they have no fear of fighting back or standing up for themselves. You hear other people make jokes about making their spouse sleep on the couch or putting him or her "in the doghouse." They talk about having huge arguments, but they don't understand that for you, a huge argument means a threat of violence. It means hours of systematic psychological torture. When I tried to tell friends and family about the fights I had with Stephen, a lot of the responses were "I would have kicked him in the balls if he laid a hand on me!" or "Why didn't you just kick him out?"

The answer is simple. I didn't want to suffer any more than I already was. More importantly, at the end of the day I didn't want to die. Being hurt or killed by your intimate partner is a real fear when they are abusive. Even though Stephen never broke my arm, instinctively I knew I was in danger every time he was angry. It wasn't until I was out of our apartment and out of the marriage that I realized how tense I had been all the time. It wasn't just walking on eggshells. I was continually denying my own feelings, planning around his rages, trying anything to keep him happy. But no matter how hard I tried, there was always something that would set him off, and I never knew how bad it was going to be.

Even though I knew the consequences, there were times I reached my limit. I don't know why dinner was such a trigger for Stephen. He found as many ways as there are recipes to make dinner a miserable experience. If dinner wasn't ready when he thought it should be, he would freak out. But if I made dinner when he normally wanted it, frequently he would refuse to eat it because he didn't feel like eating what I made. Most of the time I would just be quiet and take whatever verbal lashing he dished up for my "fuck up." Once or twice, I snapped back at him and said, "If you don't like what I cook, then make dinner yourself."

This was a mistake. There was an instant shift in his demeanor. He became quiet, his eyes went flat and gray, and his movements were slow and methodical. He walked to the refrigerator, pulled out things and took what felt like an eternity to inspect each and every one.

My stomach dropped to the very pit of my being. I felt dizzy with adrenaline because I actually had the courage to snap back while knowing that punishment was imminent. I panicked every time, knowing I needed to fix what I did, although I knew it was too late.

"I will make something else! Just tell me what you want, I can make whatever you want. Please stop, I will take care of it!" I pleaded with him. He didn't respond or even look at me. He just continued to rifle through the refrigerator, taking his time, prolonging his psychological torture.

Sometimes the blow was immediate, but other times it was like what is said about revenge: "it is a dish best served cold." The punishments were never really the same. He might choose to ignore me and keep me in suspense for days of what he was going to do. Or he could be so "annoyed" with me that he blew up at the slightest thing I would do. It took days of trying everything to get him to forgive me, and days of living in constant fear that something was going to happen, only to have nothing happen at all.

By the time I left Stephen, most of the friends I had prior to meeting him were gone. This is one of the results of being in an abusive relationship: your abuser finds ways to isolate you. He encouraged me to fight with my friends. He often twisted things they said to me into insults to upset me. One time a friend complimented my pants, and he made me believe she was actually mocking me, calling me fat. If a friend did or said something that I found questionable, he took it to the next level, fanning the flames and turning my questioning into righteous anger. Eventually I would be so angry with that friend that I would stop hanging out with her or I would act like a jerk so she would stop hanging out with me. I remember one incident around election time, Obama vs. McCain. A dear friend posted something about it on social media. I can't remember what it was now. Stephen saw it and he just laid into me about it. He was a die-hard Republican. He got me wound up and encouraged me to make my own post. I did on my page, but it was obvious I was referring to her post. She commented, "Are you talking about me?" I responded, "If the shoe fits." We didn't talk for nearly three years. That friend was Michelle, my best friend since we were twelve years old. Fortunately, now we are friends again and celebrating twenty-three years of friendship.

So, due to Stephen's efforts, I didn't have any close friends at this time. I certainly didn't have anyone that I spent time with outside of work. The only people I could spend time with were Stephen's family and about twice a year we would visit my cousin Kathy. Stephen would come with me on these visits. Kathy was the only person who was capable of handling his personality while still remaining close to me. I attribute this to the fact that she is a trained mental health professional with a Ph.D. in social work and she was able to see that I needed someone to stay in my life and remain supportive without making me feel guilty for who I married. She was a major contributor to my success in getting free of my marriage and also making it through alive.

My family didn't like Stephen. I had to try and play "peacemaker" all the time. It was exhausting. I would be excited about seeing them and dread a visit with them at the same time. It's hard to talk to people you feel are judging you negatively at every turn. With my cousin, however, I could just relax and feel accepted. The friends and family members that criticize your relationship really just end up alienating you. Often, they are trying to help and just don't understand the dynamics of an abusive relationship.

When you're finally ready to leave, you find out that you have no one. You have been ashamed for years because of how people made you feel about your partner and now you are ashamed that you failed at marriage and have to get divorced. It's a vicious cycle.

Knowing that Kathy was free of judgment made it so much easier to talk to her when things went bad. Sometimes when people talk to you about their problems, they don't want criticism or for you to tell them what you think they should do; they just want you to listen and provide support and a sympathetic ear. This is what my cousin was for me and still is. She is the type of person who wants to help and who never passes judgment. Once I decided to leave Stephen, I called her immediately and we went into action. There was no way I could have made it through all this without her support. I was lucky to have her.

I was surprised at how many other people jumped in to help me. When I got back into school and confided in a couple of my classmates, they sprang into action. I came to class the week after I left and people had gift cards for groceries, a microwave, and some small furniture items waiting for me, as I didn't take much from the house. I got my clothes and the dining room set and that was it. No one wants to ask for help or feel like they are getting charity, but everyone needs a hand sometimes. There is nothing shameful about being in trouble and needing help; it's a shame when you don't ask for it and suffer needlessly. Once you are back on your feet you can then pay it forward and help someone else in need.

In the midst of going through my divorce, I went home to Maine to visit my parents. My mother had a hard time with my attitude towards the end of my marriage. My mom is a fighter. When she believes in something, she is not afraid to fight for what she believes in until the end. She couldn't understand why I wasn't fighting to get more from Stephen. One day in the car, we had a heart to heart about it.

"Sarah, don't let him take advantage of you! You need to fight for what is yours." She was emphatic.

"Mom, I understand what you're saying, but it's not worth it," I replied in a calmer tone, trying not to argue.

"I just don't understand. You have this apartment, but you have no furniture, no TV, and he has all your things. You deserve half of everything in that old apartment." She sounded confused. She let me know she was hurt by Stephen's behavior and didn't understand it.

"It's so hard to explain, Mom," I said. "I am just so done. I am done fighting with him. I don't have the energy to do it anymore and over what? A TV? A couch? I have everything I need. I've got my clothes, my pictures, my music, and all of the things that were sentimental to me. I will save money and buy the rest when I can."

I was almost pleading with her to understand. She looked at me, concerned and bewildered. I understood she didn't want her daughter being taken advantage of. But at that time, I wasn't ready to tell her that I felt I was in danger. A TV wasn't worth my life.

Under "normal" break-up circumstances it's safe to demand the return of personal belongings, no matter how difficult it may be. However, leaving an abuser is different. Those first few months are the most dangerous. Abusers tend to take extreme action to keep their victims in the relationship.

According to statistics from the National Coalition Against Domestic Violence, "the presence of a gun in a domestic situation increases the risk of homicide by 500%." Stephen had a small arsenal in the home; he was obsessed with guns. Domestic violence organizations also caution that the most dangerous time for a victim is right after leaving. Abusers thrive on power and control, and when the victim leaves, they are losing both. In a last-ditch effort to have the power and control, they sometimes ultimately murder their victim.

I didn't have any of these statistics or this knowledge when I left. What I did have were my instincts and they told me to watch my back. The first year after leaving I was so paranoid. I never went anywhere alone if I could help it. I changed grocery stores in fear he would show up, I never went back to our favorite restaurants, I stopped going to his parents' church, and I made other adjustments to my daily routines. I tried to be unpredictable.

Except for Kathy, it sometimes felt as if I was getting a lot of judgment from people. I will never forget the day that a guy at work let me know exactly how he felt about divorce. He overheard me talking with a friend, and, uninvited, he joined our conversation.

"I never want to get divorced and be another statistic! No one tries anymore—they just get married and then get divorced when it gets hard."

This guy had no clue what was going on in my life. But his comment hit me right in my insecurities; it made me feel as though I should have tried harder. Maybe if I had cleaned better or cooked better, I wouldn't have made Stephen so angry. For a few moments I felt I was just throwing away my marriage, that I was not respecting the sanctity of marriage anymore. His words obviously cut me deep, as I remember them all these years later. I sat at my desk, and I thought about his comments for a long time. Then I got angry, and I realized he was right. I didn't want to be a statistic! But not the statistic he was talking about. I didn't want to be one of the many women still stuck in an abusive relationship. I didn't want to be one of the many women who have children in an abusive relationship. I didn't want to be one of the too many women who are beaten, and eventually killed, by an abusive husband who escalates the violence over the years. We are all a statistic of one kind or another, so I choose to be a divorcee who is alive and living a life of happiness and freedom. This is my statistic.

Divorce in an abusive relationship doesn't mean it's all over; it's just a piece of paper. The paper doesn't stop you from looking over your shoulder for the rest of your life. Stephen was so unpredictable in his moods that I constantly worried he might be triggered by something and come after me again.

Nine. *"Just tell me what you want"*

The paranoia was terrible. I never went anywhere alone in case he would show up, whether it be the grocery store or the laundromat. Every time I saw a Jeep that was a four-door Wrangler with a soft top and the same shade of green as his, my heart beat out of my chest, my stomach felt like it was going to drop at any moment, and my skin tingled as all my senses went on high alert. I knew that I couldn't live in Florida anymore, but I had a year left to finish my MBA. I planned to move back to Maine after graduation.

I figured the fear and the looking over my shoulder would magically end once I got some distance. It didn't; I was afraid that he would show up in Maine too. He had been there with me several times. We lived with my parents for two months; he knew where they lived. My mind raced each day with thoughts of the ways he could find me, and when I saw that same damn type of Jeep, I had the same feelings of terror as before.

I told myself I was being irrational; he wasn't going to come all the way to Maine to find me. But in my heart, I knew he could, and he might, and my mind would reel all over again.

In 2013 I got a Facebook message from a friend who said she ran into someone who knew Stephen at the grocery store. When she asked how Stephen was, she was told that Stephen was dying. She said that Stephen had non–Hodgkin's lymphoma. I told her that I was not aware of his condition as he and I were not in contact.

I immediately contacted Stephen's mother. "Carol, it's Sarah. I am so sorry to hear about Stephen. Are you OK?"

"What did you hear?"

I was surprised by her response, so I paused and answered as carefully as I could. "Well, I just spoke to a mutual friend who told me he had cancer, specifically non–Hodgkin's lymphoma."

Carol started crying. I could hear her trying to regain control so she could speak, but she continued crying for several minutes, while I made sympathetic noises and told her how sorry I was.

"Hold on, Sarah." I could hear her walking across the kitchen, and I imagined her grabbing the box of tissues on the counter. "Roger and I knew he was sick. We just didn't know what he had. Oh, this is awful." She cried for a few more minutes and then told me the story of the last time they saw Stephen.

In October 2012, they met with him for lunch at a restaurant. He told them he had gone to the doctor. The doctor said Stephen's white blood cell count was a little off and he wanted to do further testing.

She said they both tried to ask him more questions, but he refused to say anything more about it. Which doctor? Where was he getting tested? What kind of tests? He didn't answer one question and, finally, he stormed out of the restaurant. As Roger and Carol were leaving, a woman sitting at the table to next to them stopped her and said, "I'm a nurse and I overheard your conversation. Sorry, but I just want you to know that what he said doesn't sound right. He should get a second opinion." Stephen and his parents said their goodbyes in the parking lot. This was the last time they would see their son for almost a year.

Carol said they tried to follow up with him. They called and texted, but received no answers. They called his work and he wouldn't answer or call back. Finally, after a couple months they drove to his apartment and found he had moved, leaving no forwarding address. They drove to his place of work, but he wasn't there and no one could or would give them his address.

Eventually, he called them. He had moved in with a doctor who was a friend and customer of his. At some point Stephen reached out to his aunt Deborah and they met up for dinner. Often, he would reach out to her whenever he needed money. He told Deborah that he had been accepted into some experimental treatment program that cost $750,000. Then he went radio silent again. He eventually resurfaced. In October 2013 he said had been diagnosed with non–Hodgkin's lymphoma and undergone the experimental treatments and was now cured.

I knew that Stephen lied about things, from small things to large. And although it felt strange to think so, I started to wonder if he had cancer at all. It sounded like something he would come up with to manipulate someone. Whoever the intended target was, I didn't know. But none of the information added up. Although people are diagnosed with cancer every day, nothing about Stephen's story made sense. I could see him getting something out of faking an illness. I felt a bit uncharitable for being suspicious, but I had known Stephen. And I knew what he was capable of.

At the end of 2014 Stephen was fired from his job at Musician Central. Another mutual friend contacted me and told me that he had stolen a guitar for his girlfriend. When they broke up, Stephen tried to sneak the guitar back into inventory. When he did this he was caught by the company and fired for internal theft. Even two years after our divorce people reached out to me to share news of my ex-husband. Part of me wished they wouldn't, but part of me was validated by these stories. It confirmed what I knew and what I suspected about Stephen.

Nine. *"Just tell me what you want"*

While we were married Stephen was in control of most things, including the mail. We always lived in apartments where you get one key to a mailbox. I didn't think anything of letting him have the mailbox key. It was extremely easy for him to hide all of the bills from me, bills in my name that I knew nothing about. I didn't find out until I went to finance a car after I left Stephen and he wouldn't let me have the Honda Civic anymore. When the dealership checked my credit, my 780 credit score was now at 420. I went home and pulled up my credit report online to see what had happened. My credit had been destroyed by years of bad debt and I hadn't known it.

The laptop his company gave him when he became a GM was actually mine. Stephen stole my Social Security number, went on the Dell website, and financed it in my name, without my knowing. He had it shipped to his work, and when he brought it home, he lied. I remembered how nice the laptop was, and how surprised I was that Musician Central was giving their managers top-of-the-line gaming computers. It was a $3,000 laptop, financed in my name and not one payment made. I never saw the bills or the many notices from collection agencies because I didn't have the mailbox key. He purchased countless other items under my name, totaling around $30,000. It took me four years to make settlements and get payments to the creditors. I couldn't prove he did this without my consent, so when I filed for divorce, I asked for at least 50 percent of it to be paid by him. The judge said that while he was granting me my request, the only way I would actually get it was if I sued Stephen for it. I didn't have the money for an attorney to help me with my divorce, let alone one to help me sue him for that money. So I dealt with it. After I finally paid it all off, I hired a credit attorney who assisted me with getting all of my credit reports cleaned up.

Now that I knew that he was capable of anything, I took measures to keep my location hidden from him. My driver's license had my parents' address on it. My thoughts were that if he tried to find me, he would go to their house and my dad would intercept him. When I filed for divorce, I used my aunt and uncle's address in Florida because they lived in the same county, and I didn't want him to have the address of my new apartment. I made his parents and his aunt promise never to share the address with Stephen.

In 2013, I got an email from him. He was applying for a business loan, and he needed copies of all of our prior years' tax returns. I had to calm myself down from the panic attack after seeing his name flash on my computer screen. Then I thought about the ramifications of sending him this information. This man already committed financial crimes against me using my SSN, and if I sent him these documents, he would again have access to my private information. I reached out to an attorney and asked for advice. The attorney me that if he really needed the old returns, he could just call the IRS and it would send him copies. I emailed him back and told him that I would send him the documents if he would send me $15,000, his half of the $30,000 in bad debt. I was proud of myself for standing up to him. The next day I got an email back from him: "Once I get the documents and I get the loan I will have the money to send you."

Well, at least I tried. Lessons having been learned, I did not respond. I also never sent him the documents. He never pursued it again.

Even before my conversation with Nick and my decision to investigate my own life, I started researching anti-social personality disorders. Based on what I learned from my therapist and my cousin Kathy, I knew there was more going on with Stephen. He had no sense of empathy for others, and he didn't care if what he did or said would hurt anyone else; he only cared about himself. He also had traits of narcissistic personality disorder. I read narcissists frequently have feelings of unworthiness and powerlessness underneath their grand façade. To maintain their false image they often lie, steal, and cheat to sustain their grandiose but completely fabricated identity. The extreme cases of NPD can lead to violence, such as stalking, battering, murder, and, contrary to popular belief, suicide.

I wanted to understand Stephen's and my marriage, so I continued reading. In the *Diagnostic and Statistical Manual of Mental Disorders* (or *DSM-5*) I found a succinct overview of behaviors people with anti-social personality disorders display. As I read through the list, I recognized many of the things Stephen would do or say during our marriage. For example, I noticed Stephen was a very cold person who was unemotional even during the toughest of situations.

We often use humor when faced with stress. Early on I thought he was using humor to cope with difficult news, but soon I realized it was his way of manipulating others by drawing attention to himself and away from anyone else or the situation at hand. Stephen had a very grandiose view of himself. He thought of himself as very intelligent and was quick to remind me how smart he was and how his opinions were all that mattered, regardless of the topic.

Stephen was not the type of person who had friends he remained close with throughout his life. I never knew of friends from high school or any friend that lasted long. Friends to him were pawns used to get access to things he wanted, whether that be power or money. When things weren't going well with Stephen and me, he would threaten or intimidate me to make sure I didn't call my parents or others for help. Stephen viewed his everyday behavior as normal. In his mind he was perfect. It was everyone around him who had problems, especially me.

I recognize that it is not my place to "diagnose" Stephen. I was simply figuring out who my ex-husband was. Who, exactly, had I been married to? Stephen was a perpetual liar. He constantly deceived others by proclaiming to have things that we didn't have or bragging about things he had never done. Most of these lies or fantasies were designed to make him look better than he was. He had a total disrespect for social norms or laws.

My cousin offered to take us on a tour of the Pentagon in the post–9/11 era, when the security to get into the building was very tight. My cousin and I observed that Stephen got highly agitated and borderline aggressive while we waited in line to enter the building. Stephen then used "humor," saying, "I think I will take out my AK-47 now," drawing attention to himself, saying it loud enough for people around us to hear. Stephen had no regard for societal norms like paying bills or professional responsibilities. He often went to work late and was sloppy with his work responsibilities. Stephen's parents loved him deeply, yet when things were rough in their relationship, he never felt any guilt or remorse. He couldn't see things from their point of view or how their feelings might have been hurt. Even on Christmas Day, when we went to meet them for breakfast, he was agitated and cold to all of them when they were dealing with the emergency of his grandfather's fall.

I came to believe I was married to a sociopath. But I only had my foggy memories and friends' observations to back up this feeling. Later my suspicions were confirmed and even I was shocked.

Ten

"We were worried about Stephen"

The day after I read Nick's article on LinkedIn, I started retracing my steps. I went back to the beginning and tried to unravel all I knew about Stephen and my time with him. Nick had shared his Google drive files with me, containing the criminal records from Florida and Colorado. But Nick didn't have the police records from Lake City, describing the day Stephen died. I don't know why, but I felt it was important for me to know more about his death. That feeling of having a close call hovered over me and I couldn't shake it. I took a deep breath and called the Lake City Police Department, requesting the death investigation records. They said I could expect them by the end of the day via email. While I waited, I thought back to the day his mother called me.

February 25, 2016, I was at home, talking on the phone with a friend when I saw I had another call. "Carol Jones." Since I was on the phone, I didn't answer. She left a voicemail, and I got a weird feeling. She never called me at that time of night, and it had been a while since we had spoken, so the call seemed very random. I quickly got off the phone with my friend and listened to the voicemail.

"Hi, Sarah, it's Mom. Something happened to Stephen. Can you please call me back?"

Her voice was calm, so I wasn't too concerned about what she wanted to tell me. In fact, I was annoyed. Why did she think I want to know anything about Stephen? We made an agreement when I divorced her son that in order for me to stay in her life, we wouldn't talk about him and she could never talk to him about me. I was half-expecting her to tell me he was getting married or something like that. I decided to call her back anyway but she didn't answer. As I started to leave a message she called back.

"Hey, Mom. What happened to Stephen?" I was not prepared for what she said next.

84

Ten. "We were worried about Stephen"

"His body was found in the woods. It's either homicide or suicide."

"Oh my God, I am so sorry! When did this happen?" I felt dizzy and disoriented.

"We don't know. Sometime today, a hiker found his body." Her voice started to crack.

"Where are you? Who is with you?" I asked, concerned that she was alone and upset.

"I am home. Everyone is here. Grandpa, Roger, his brother, sister-in-law, their kids, and Deborah. We are all sitting in the living room just waiting. The police officer sent Roger home and said he would be here soon."

"Sent Roger home?" I asked, totally confused.

"Yes, we were worried about Stephen as we hadn't been able to reach him all day so Roger went to look for him. When he got to the place where Stephen went hiking, he came up on a crime scene. The police told him it was Stephen. They said that a hiker found his body and called the police and that it was either a homicide or suicide and is under investigation. They said they would send someone to the house to talk to us and then told Roger to come home."

She didn't really have any additional details and at this point she was sobbing. I offered more condolences and told her to keep in contact and I would call her tomorrow to check on her.

We hung up, and I immediately called my mother. After I talked to my mother, I was still reeling and decided that I needed to talk to Kathy. We were both in shock and disbelief. Kathy worked in the field of suicide prevention. We both thought it was unbelievable that Stephen, the most narcissistic person we knew, would kill himself. Kathy started to ask questions related to some of the typical signs that would show a person is suicidal. I didn't know any answers, but this gave me good questions to ask his family in a follow-up conversation. We talked about the possibility of a homicide as the cause of death. This, we could believe. Stephen was always scheming and screwing people over. We could imagine him crossing the wrong person.

As I was going over the details of that night in my mind for the millionth time, I was interrupted by the ding on my laptop indicating a new email had come in. It was the email from the Lake City Police Department. I stared at it for a moment. Was I ready for this? What would I find? What clues was I *hoping* to find? I opened the documents and started to read.

The report was a little hard to follow as there were several different parties mentioned. Please be advised that the following paragraphs include a graphic description of a victim of suicide.

Full Investigation Report: February 25, 2016, at 5:42 p.m.

County Sheriff's office responded to a park/nature preserve in Florida as the result of a 911 call reporting a deceased person. After looking at the scene they contacted the office and requested a detective come out to open an investigation. The detective arrived on scene about an hour later at 6:45 p.m. The rest of the report is written from the point of view of the detective leading the investigation.

Deputies arrived at the park and were led to the scene by one of the parties who found the deceased person. Deputies observed the body and their initial comments were that they observed the deceased person lying on the ground with an apparent gunshot wound to the head. They observed a black handgun near the decedent's right knee. At this time, they located his wallet and ID to identify the decedent as Stephen Jones.

The detective was introduced to the man who called in to report the deceased person, the reportee. Reportee advised that he arrived at the park alone at about 3:30 p.m. He walked to the "outer trail" and while walking he saw the decedent. He advised that he spoke to the man and said "Hey, how you doing?" The decedent just nodded his head slightly but did not respond verbally. Reportee continued walking and at about 4:50 p.m. he received a phone call from a friend letting him know that they just arrived at the park to join him on his walk. Reportee walked back to the park entrance to meet his friend. Reportee and his friend decided to walk the "two mile loop" together. While walking they saw the decedent lying on the ground near a wooden bench. The detective asked the reportee to describe what he saw.

"The guy's head was by the bench with his lower body extended away from the bench. I noticed blood on his hands and there was a black handgun near his knee area. I am not familiar with guns so I can't tell you what kind it was, but I do know that it was not a revolver. I also noticed a pair of sunglasses a couple feet away from the guy's feet and a hat lying on the ground as well. I did not hear any loud noises or hear a gunshot prior to finding the body."

Reportee called 911 at about 5:15 p.m. While standing near the decedent waiting for the police arrive 2 other groups of people were walking towards them on the trail. One of the groups had 2 adults and 3 children and the other was 2 adults with a dog. The reportee and his friend intercepted the groups and advised them to turn around so they wouldn't see the body or disrupt the scene. When the police were arriving on the scene the friend went to meet them and led them to the scene. The reportee remained with the body.

The detective then interviewed the friend of the reportee. She advised that she arrived at the park to meet her friend for a walk on the trails. Her friend came to the gate to meet her and they started walking on the trail to the "right." She said she never heard any loud noises or gunshots. While they were walking they came upon the decedent lying on his back on the ground in front of a bench. She said she saw blood on his hand but couldn't recall which hand. She saw a black handgun lying on the ground near his right leg, sunglasses with a lens missing and a hat a few feet away from the decedent's feet. She said her friend called 911 (Reportee) and advised the 2 groups of walkers to turn around as one group had kids and the other group had a dog. She advised that she and her friend never left the trail and they did not touch the body or any of the items they observed on the ground. Her friend stayed with the body and she ran to the "railroad" to flag down and direct emergency responders to the location.

While taking the statement from the "friend" the detective noticed another man walking in the park carrying only a backpack. The approached the man and interviewed him. They only referred to this person as "Other Man" in the report. This man had been fishing in the park and was on his way out when he came upon the investigators and the scene. There is a small side investigation in the report as the man claimed to be fishing but had no fishing gear on him when he came upon the scene. After a little investigation it was determined that he had ditched his gear because he was afraid he would get in trouble for fishing in a nature preserve. The police followed him to where he hid the fishing pole and tackle box and determined he was not involved and allowed him to leave.

Officers conducted gunshot residue testing on the Reportee, friend, and Other Man. All were negative.

At around 7:21 p.m. the detective contacted the decedent's parents, Roger Jones and Carol Jones. They were in the parking lot area of the park. Roger and Carol were distraught so the detective decided to allow them to be interviewed together. They did not want to be separated.

Roger advised the detective that he is the biological father of the decedent and provided a statement.

"At around 4:37 p.m. I received several text messages and telephone calls from my son's girlfriend, Angela Plourde, who lives in Colorado. In the messages and calls she said that she was concerned for Stephen. She said that he had sent her several Facebook messages about 'giving up' and 'not being able to take it anymore.' She then sent me a Google Maps image of a park that Stephen had sent to her saying this is where he will be. With the map image she sent me, we started to try and find Stephen. We initially went to the wrong park and then came to this one when we realized he wasn't at the other location. When arrived here we saw that you were already on the scene."

The detective asked him when he last saw his son and he advised that it was the previous evening. "He seemed ok, just tired and he didn't want to make dinner like he had been over the last several weeks."

When the detective asked if there was any reason why Stephen would want to hurt himself his father replied, "Approximately 4 weeks ago, Stephen had moved to Colorado to be with his girlfriend. The day after he arrived, he was arrested on fraud charges from Florida. My son was 'caged' for the next 6 days on his way back to Florida. When he got back to Florida, my wife and I bonded him out of jail, and he has been staying with us since then. The fraud charges came from one of Stephen's longtime friends and I believe that is why he was so 'stressed.'"

Next the detective took a statement from Carol Jones, and she confirmed that she is the biological mother of the decedent.

"I last saw Stephen this morning at around 7:00 a.m. He was still in bed at our home. I spoke with him, and he seemed 'normal.' I left to run some errands and when I got back home around 10:00 a.m., his Jeep was not there, and he was not at home."

Roger and Carol told the detective that Stephen did not have a history of mental illness and had never threatened or attempted suicide. When asked if Stephen owned any firearms, they advised that he did own a black handgun that he kept in his Jeep. They advised they noticed it when they flew to Colorado to collect his belongings and drove the Jeep back to Florida.

This was a lot of information to take in. Reading through the report and the statements was certainly an emotional experience for me. I'm a very detail-oriented person, and what stuck out the most is that both Roger and Carol were interviewed at the scene. Carol told me that she wasn't at the scene, that Roger was there by himself and that he came home to tell her Stephen was dead, and that then the detective came to the house to interview her. That said, it is entirely possible she just mixed up her facts during the shock and trauma of what had just happened. Another thing that hit me right in the gut was the timeline of events. Stephen by all accounts was deceased by around 5:30 p.m., his parents were on the scene after the detective arrived, so around 7:00 p.m., and the phone call I received was at around 7:30 p.m. I just don't fully understand why they called me within an hour of finding out their son was gone. We had been divorced just over three years and we hadn't spoken in months. I would have expected a call the next day or week but not within hours.

Around 8:00 p.m. the CSI team arrived on the scene. According to its report it

observed the decedent lying on his back with his upper body slightly twisted to the left. His head was facing south with his feet extended to the north. There was a large amount of blood near the decedent's head. Near his right knee area, they observed a black in color, .45 caliber semiautomatic handgun. A pair of sunglasses which was missing one lens and a hat were near the decedent's feet. The hat was observed to have a bullet hole on each side—the hole on the right side had powder burns present and both holes had hair present which was consistent in length and color to the decedent's hair. A single lens, apparently from the sunglasses, was located approximately ten feet east of the decedent's body. The firearm was checked and was found to have blowback evidence present on the muzzle. There was no magazine present in the firearm's magazine well, nor was there one present on scene. The firearm was found to be empty with no ammunition present. One single spent shell casing was found approximately thirty feet—across the walking trail—south of the decedent's body. A paper map of the park was located approximately forty feet southwest of the decedent's body. The decedent's body was checked. A gunshot wound was present on the right side of his head with an apparent exit wound on the left side. There was apparent blowback evidence on his right hand. No other trauma was observed on the decedent's body. During check of the decedent's body, a wallet, pocketknife, and set of keys were located. No other items were found.

His body was picked up and taken to the ME's office at around 8:10 p.m.

Around 9:30 p.m. after a search of Stephen's Jeep by the officers, they contacted Carol Jones via telephone to have her and Roger some back to the scene to take possession of the decedent's Jeep. Also, at that time, Stephen's wallet and contents (excluding his Florida driver's license and social security card), his pocketknife, and his keys were turned over to the Joneses.

On February 26, 2016, an autopsy on Stephen's body was conducted at the medical examiner's office. The autopsy advised that the decedent suffered a contact gunshot wound of the head. The projectile traveled from right to left and slightly front to back. The projectile exited the left side of the head and was not recovered. Cause of Death was Gunshot Wound of the Head, and the Manner of Death was Suicide.

The final note on the report stated, "Case Status: Closed/Suicide."

I didn't think I would have such a strong reaction to reading the report. It shocked me. The gun he used was the first gun I ever shot. He taught me how to use it. I had fired the gun he used to kill himself. That stunned me. It was just too close. He loved that gun; it was the first gun he ever owned. The CSI notes really hit me. There was a section about putting bags over his head. It was desperately sad that a human life ended as evidence in an investigation. I could actually see his face and his body in my mind when I read the description from the CSI report. The reaction was subtle at first, just a flip in my stomach, then I felt my hands start to shake, and eventually I cried.

I couldn't help but put myself in the shoes of his parents. Getting an alert to go check on their son, probably expecting to find him OK, and then driving up to a crime scene … their worst fears realized. My heart just hurt to think about the entire situation.

Stronger Than That

After I read the Lake City records, I needed time to absorb them, but then I went back to the files on Nick's Google drive. I discovered that Stephen was hired in late 2013 to be the office manager, bookkeeper, and personal assistant to a doctor. He met the doctor while he was managing Musician Central. When Stephen was fired from Musician Central, he agreed to work for this man and help him start up his own medical practice. Due to the nature of the position, the doctor gave Stephen full access to his personal and company financial records. In late December of 2015, Stephen left on a vacation to Colorado, and while he was on this vacation, the doctor discovered that he was being defrauded by Stephen. The following is a summary of what happened based on the investigation reports from the county sheriff's office.

As the doctor's personal assistant, Stephen was in charge of managing the money involving his upcoming business. He had even moved into the doctor's home. One can just imagine the stories he was spinning.

Stephen gained access to a bank account that was in the doctor's name during that time. All of the mail regarding finances and billing statements were then intercepted by Stephen daily and sorted before being distributed to the doctor. Reading this, I realized he was doing the same thing to the doctor he did to me. The doctor trusted Stephen and wasn't suspicious of this routine.

On December 18, 2015, Stephen left to see his girlfriend, Angela Plourde, in Colorado and was due to return on January 1, 2016. Three days after Stephen left, the doctor checked his mail and found a bank billing statement for a Visa card with his name on it. He opened the statement and noticed that Stephen's name was also on the account and Stephen listed as an authorized user.

He started to look through the charges and found purchases that he never made for firearms, plane tickets, insurance payments, and various dining expenses. He noticed that the credit limit on this card was $30,000, a limit much higher than he had authorized. He immediately contacted Stephen via text message to find out what was going on. Stephen initially replied that he was aware of the charges. He said there must have been a mistake at the bank. The doctor sent him a picture of the bill. Stephen replied immediately, asking him not to contact law enforcement. He said he would sell the firearms he purchased and hire an attorney with his father to repay the doctor.

The doctor wasn't interested in what Stephen had to say. He had already called law enforcement and cancelled the card immediately. He started to dig around some more, wondering what else he might discover. He found two bins in the home that had several bank statements as well as several statements and receipts of gold for cash trade-ins. The doctor was in the habit of buying gold to trade and kept it in his safety deposit box at a bank. Through the police investigation it was discovered that Stephen set up a safety deposit box at the same bank in the same location as the doctor's box. Stephen had access to the key to the box through the safe in the doctor's home and was able to gain access to it while under the guise of accessing his own safety deposit box. He would then take gold and silver out of the doctor's box and trade it in for cash.

One had to give Stephen credit: he was good at being an evil genius, but like most people with those traits, he always took things too far. The doctor also found a document with his signature forged on it. It was a fake letterhead made to look like his company asked to have the Visa card limit increased from $10,000 to $30,000. The contact information and email on the bottom of the letter belonged to Stephen. He not only had control of the mail but also had set up the online billing accounts for them, so the doctor did not have any access to monitor these accounts. The doctor noticed Stephen had taken many long-distance trips and had purchased several firearms. He thought it was weird, but Stephen always said these things were either gifts from his dad or he had just been saving up, which was the exact same thing he used to say to me.

In addition to the bank account Stephen also gained access to the doctor's other investment accounts. Somehow Stephen transferred $17,000 from the doctor's retirement account to his personal bank account and then transferred it to his corporate bank account. It appeared the purpose was to pay down the fraudulent debt racked up by Stephen on the corporate account. Through text messages Stephen admitted that he had defrauded the doctor of approximately $175,000 in credit card debt and another $100,000 in the loss of gold and silver from the safety deposit box.

At one point Stephen texted, "I'm not going to deny anything." Again, Stephen asked the doctor to not get law enforcement involved and promised that he would pay him back. Stephen informed the doctor that he was having a trust fund set up and would mail him a check for his loss. He told the doctor that he was in Lake City with his mother and his dying grandfather and that his mother wanted him to accompany his grandfather's body to Jerusalem for burial. Stephen was in Colorado and his grandfather was very much alive and not dying at this time.

A warrant was issued, and Stephen was arrested in Colorado on January 15, 2016, and was detained in a county jail. He was later transported to a Florida county jail, arriving on February 8, 2016. Stephen was released on $25,000 bond.

It's hard to describe how I felt when reading through these documents. After our divorce, whenever I tried sharing my experiences with Stephen with anyone, I was met with disbelief. Those years changed me, they defined me, they made me stronger against my will. But whenever I tried to explain what it was like being married to Stephen, very few people believed me. Now everyone knew the truth.

My husband used my identity to finance tens of thousands of dollars of purchases in my name and then hid it from me. People thought I was lying or just plain stupid. Many of my friends didn't believe me. The police and debt collectors told me to prove it, and I couldn't. It was his word against mine. I had no redress. But the doctor wasn't married to Stephen, and when he brought his evidence to the police, he was believed. This was a doctor—a surgeon, no less—a person everyone can agree is smart, a person you would think would not be susceptible to such things, and yet he too fell victim to Stephen's manipulations.

I felt vindicated. I am not a liar. I am not stupid. As odd as it sounds, given the roller coaster of emotions I was on, I simply cannot express how happy and excited this made me.

After he was bailed out, Stephen was living at home, figuring out what to do next. He wasn't working. His girlfriend Angela was still in Colorado.

The story his parents told me was a little different from the police report. His mother told me that he had spoken to her on his last morning as she left for work. He seemed in good spirits. He texted with his girlfriend and told her he was going hiking on the trail behind his old high school. His mom told me that he and the girlfriend were texting most of that day. According to Angela, the texts seemed normal.

Around 6 that night Angela called Stephen's parents and asked if they had heard from him. He hadn't replied to her in several hours and she was getting concerned. His parents had not heard from him either, so Roger went to look for Stephen where he had gone hiking.

According to Roger, when he got to the hiking trail, he saw Stephen's Jeep as well as a bunch of police cars and an entire crime scene set up with a caution tape perimeter. When Roger approached the perimeter, an officer came up and asked him to back away. Roger asked him what was going on, as he was there looking for his son. The officer asked Roger what his name was and he replied, "Roger Jones." The officer asked him if he knew a Stephen Jones. Roger replied, "Yes, that's my son." The officer advised Roger that a hiker heard a gunshot and then came upon Stephen's body on a bench on the path.

Roger was told they were investigating to determine if the wound was self-inflicted or not. They asked Roger to go home and advised that someone would be over to talk to them that night. It would take a couple days, but the investigation confirmed that he ended his life by suicide at sunset on a park bench. As I recalled these details of Stephen's last hours, I thought back to the stark descriptions in the police report: "The victim is wearing grey athletic pants with apparent blood, a grey athletic jacket with apparent blood, grey and red tennis shoes and a green and black scarf with apparent blood. I observed apparent gunshot wounds to the left and right sides of the victim's head. I observed apparent blood on the victim's face, neck, left hand and right hand...."

Stephen was dead.

At the time, it was almost impossible for me to process. I didn't know what to think or what to feel. I was upset for his family. They were in shock. We talked often over the next few days, which was bizarre and difficult for me. His mother called constantly, telling me every little detail. When they went down to identify the body, she told me how cold he was to the touch. She even told me they all joked about Stephen always loving being cold. This made me uncomfortable. Another time she and Roger called laughing hysterically, telling me how tacky the floral decorations were at the funeral home and how weird the undertaker was. I understood later this was simple gallows humor, but it reminded me of how Stephen responded to emotional situations in the past, always passing over things with "humor."

It was impossible to get any real information from them. I didn't even know it was a suicide or that the gunshot was to the head for days after they found out. It felt as if they were deliberately directing a narrative that they wanted to be true.

As much as he had done to me, when I found out the way he died, it affected me deeply. A single gunshot wound to the head. I felt so sick to my stomach that he would feel that things were so awful that his only option was to take his own life, that there was no way out. It broke my heart.

I also felt awkward feeling that way because I felt like I would be judged for my sorrow. I felt like I should hate him and be glad he was dead, and a part of me does believe that the world is a better place without people like him in it.

But it is so easy to say in abstract that you wish someone was dead … but then do you really? Wouldn't that make you just like him if that was true of you? When he was alive, I wished that he wouldn't be happier than me in life, but I never wished him sorrow to the point of suicide, and I never wished him death.

There was to be a memorial service for Stephen. His parents asked me to come.

I told them that I just couldn't make it down there. I didn't have vacation time at work, and I didn't have the money for a flight. I gave every excuse I could come up with. There was no way in hell I was going to that memorial service. How could I? I couldn't go to a place where people would be mourning the death and sharing happy memories of the man who tormented me for so many years. I was kind of shocked his parents would ask me. They knew how bad our relationship was. They may have been in denial about any physical abuse, but I had spoken to them numerous times about his verbal abuse and his temper, looking for advice on how to handle their son.

A few weeks later, Stephen's aunt sent me a link to a YouTube video of the memorial. I remember not wanting to watch it. I imagined photos of him all around, and people pretending he was a good man, so I didn't open the link for several months. Eventually curiosity got the best of me. The first thing that caught my attention was how many empty seats there were. How could a man who boasted about having so many friends die and have so few people actually show up to his service?

Watching the ceremony, I was shocked that the stories people told about him as "fond" memories were actually mean things he had done to them. His brother, for example, told this story: "I had gotten a bonus at work of $500 and decided that I wanted to do something nice for my whole family as I don't normally have the money to do that. I took everyone out for dinner at Olive Garden. Stephen came and in typically larger than life Stephen fashion he ordered the most expensive Scotch on the menu, the most expensive meal on the menu, and the most expensive dessert on the menu. Most of the bill for dinner was just to pay for Stephen's meal! He was always playing jokes like that."

What a horrible thing to do. Your brother, who is the father of three young kids, with only one income for his family, who lives with your aunt due to financial troubles, takes the entire family out to dinner (nine people including the kids) and you order the most expensive *everything* on the menu?! What's worse is that this was the only story your brother could come up with to tell at your memorial service. His brother asked a friend to play a song for the memorial and it was a song that Stephen hated. It's just so sad. His family didn't even really know him.

Eleven

The Other Woman

When I talked to Nick, he mentioned several people who reached out to him about his article. Denise was not among them. At the beginning of my "investigation," I made a list of people who might talk with me about Stephen. I sent out inquiries, and now I was waiting to hear back. In the meantime, I found Denise on Instagram.

I always had the suspicion that Stephen was messing around with one of his employees, but I never knew for certain if he had an affair. Denise was in college at a local performing arts school and worked part-time in the sales department at Musician Central with Stephen.

She often called or texted him at 2 o'clock in the morning. I would wake to the blip of a text message. He would get out of bed, put on some clothes, and walk through the apartment, and then I would hear the door open and close. When he returned, I asked, "Is everything OK?" He usually said it was someone from the store with an issue and he didn't want to wake me. Sometimes he said it was an alarm at the store. One time he actually told me it was Denise from work, and she was in crisis due to family issues or some mental health issues, and he was just trying to be there for his employee.

He frequently told me how beautiful she was, always going on about her exotic Lebanese ethnicity and the fact she was a tattoo model featured in *Inked* magazine. He reminded me that I was overweight and made me feel bad about my weight gain over the years of being married. I felt terrible about myself anyway and I was starting to hate her.

I never had the courage to come right out and ask him if he was cheating, even though I was sure he was. He lied about everything, so asking would have been useless anyway. At times, I was incredibly angry. At other times, I could care less that he cheated, and later I was actually happy he cheated. I know this sounds strange but seeing him care about someone more than me gave me a little edge of courage to leave. It gave me hope that I hadn't had before, hope that if I left, he wouldn't come after me because he had someone new to focus on. As incredible as it seems to me now, it wasn't totally clear in my mind that I wasn't the problem. He had me convinced that if I acted better, he would be nicer to me. In my mind, this girl was prettier, skinnier, nicer, and more outgoing than me, so she would get the nice and kind Stephen. But years later I realized that wasn't true and then I actually felt a measure of guilt for leaving him to her, like you would feel if you left a ticking time bomb with someone as a birthday gift. I knew by then that no matter how much "better" one acted, the cruel Stephen would always emerge.

So now, in search of all the answers, I had Denise's Instagram. How do you message a woman and ask her if she had an affair with your husband? At this point in my life, I had no ill feelings towards her, but would she believe me? Putting myself in her shoes, I felt like I would have zero interest in talking. Naturally, I would assume the wife wanted to attack me both physically and verbally. With this in mind I knew that I needed to word my initial message in a way that would show her I was not mad and just wanted to know what happened. What did I have to lose? Nothing. She didn't have to answer, and in the worst-case scenario, she cussed me out via DM. I've been through worse, right?

When I found her page, I knew it was her right away. She looked very much the same. I distinctly remember the pictures that Stephen showed me. She was very thin and had tattoos all down her body, from her neck down to her feet. She had straight black hair. I remembered the first picture he showed me; she was naked except for a thong and a fur coat that was open, exposing her entire front but with her breasts covered. In the second photo she was in a bikini or maybe a bra and underwear, I can't remember for sure. When I found her Instagram, it was full of similar photos of her. She was still modeling and gorgeous and confident, two things I never felt I was, so I could see why Stephen was drawn to her. There were a lot of pictures of her art and pictures of her with her friends. She seemed to be living her best life, which made me happy that Stephen obviously hadn't ruined this woman too. I finally stopped snooping and sent her a message.

> Hi, Denise, so you don't know me but I am Stephen Jones's former wife. I know that you worked for him at Musician Central and I am doing research for a memoir I'm writing about my life with Stephen. I expect that you may not reply to this message, but I am curious about your relationship with him. I was told by some of the guys that he had stopped wearing his wedding ring at work and most new employees (especially women) didn't even know

he was married. I caught him talking with you late at night on FB messenger and trying to hide it from me. Taking late night phone calls from a mystery woman that he could only take outside our apartment. I have just always been curious if he was dating you while we were married. If you're comfortable answering I would appreciate it and if not, I completely understand that as well. Best wishes to you either way!!

Message sent. Now all I could do was wait. Ten minutes later I got a response ... my heart was racing.

Hi Sarah, I appreciate you reaching out and want to give you my most sincere condolences for Stephen's loss. I can't imagine how hard these last few years must have been for you and of course his family. I also want to be as honest and open with you as I can be because you deserve that. Stephen and I never shared anything physical, and my intentions were never romantic. I think we grew close over the time we worked together and developed a connection, but I only ever wanted a strong friendship with Stephen. I have to say that I was much younger then and lacked a lot of understanding and awareness at that age and handled relationships pretty poorly.

I sat back in my chair, a little surprised. I don't know what I was expecting, but it wasn't this. I had made snap judgments based on her appearance and my pain when Stephen and I were married. I found myself admiring her honest self-appraisal. I wondered what other revelations were in store as I read on.

I am very sorry if that caused issues or overlapped in your marriage and can't apologize enough for causing you any stress or pain. I know Stephen loved you deeply. I also think he was lost and unsure of what he wanted in his life. I often think about how poorly I handled things. Sometimes I even take responsibility for causing Stephen to lose his path in life and ultimately blame myself for some of his pain. I know that's a really stupid and self-involved idea to have, but I get really sad trying to figure out where his pain might've come from. I also beat myself up about how my friendship with Stephen might've looked then, and if I hadn't entered his life, he may have remained happily married to you, his beautiful and loyal wife.

Hearing her talk about my marriage as "happy" or how much Stephen loved me hit a nerve. I wanted to vomit. I would rather have heard she had sex with him in my bed with me in the next room. I wanted to be angry with her, but reading on, it became clear she was another one of Stephen's victims.

In any case, I apologize deeply. I hope you are able to recognize that the intentions were never to hurt anyone. You are so kind, and so was Stephen, and I will never forgive myself for causing a bit of a mess for anyone. I think Stephen was searching for something he needed within himself and got lost a few times along that journey. I think we were strong in our friendship, and

I think Stephen was looking for happiness in any place he could possibly find it. Maybe he thought for a moment it would be in me? But I was not that place, and his job and marriage weren't those places, because the place he needed to find it most was within himself. I'm sorry for rambling. I just want you to fully understand that I never meant to cause anyone any hurt.

I finished reading and then immediately read her message again. Reading over it a second time, I had a mixture of feelings come up that didn't completely make sense to me. First, I felt bad for her. She had been hurting just like me all these years. She had fallen into the vortex that was Stephen Jones's charm: "Woe is me, I'm a wounded puppy, and I'm so deep, please stroke my ego and tell me I'm amazing."

She even thought she had a role to play in his being so unhappy that he ended his own life. But in addition to feeling bad for her, I was mad. Furious, even. Her belief she affected his life so much reminded me of Nick. I felt like another person was stealing my story. I decided to set her straight.

Thanks for responding, I really appreciate it. Let me try and relieve some of this guilt. Stephen was not the person he pretended to be in public. He was an abusive and hurtful man. He abused me emotionally at every opportunity and tormented me daily. He flaunted his relationship with you in my face because I was overweight and a piece of shit, as he would say. He would kick and hit me and eventually really attacked me. I ran away and never spoke to him again. Stephen had many demons. He committed crimes against me financially that took me years to recover from.

Eventually he was caught committing similar crimes against a man he called a friend who employed him as his assistant. He was facing many years in prison for those crimes and that is what led to his death.

I truly hope his friendship to you was real. I just don't believe he was actually capable of it … honestly seeing him talking to you and thinking he loved someone else helped me find the strength to escape. I was so worried that if I left, he would hunt me down, but seeing him in love with someone else made me realize he didn't care about me at all … as if the words and beating didn't do that already.

After telling her the truth about Stephen and my life with him, I felt a bit better, but I was nervous for her reaction. I didn't have long to wait.

God, Sarah, I am so sorry. I had absolutely no idea. And I hate to hear that. I came out of an incredibly abusive relationship just over a year ago and can say that I understand the pain of it. I cared about Stephen as my friend, but I can't even say we were close enough for me to sense any of that. I knew he was very personable around people and that it couldn't be entirely genuine. I always gave people the benefit of the doubt at that time. Like I said I was young, naive, and careless at that age. Once I started dating someone while Stephen and I were growing close, and I noticed him acting strange. He would drive past my boyfriend's house, being a bit aggressive, but again, I never let him in to my life so closely that I could even see a dark side.

I know he treated doc unfairly in the end, and now I see that he didn't deserve a wife like you from the start. I hope that this can at least provide some closure for you. Or peace of mind. I am very sorry you ever had to go through that. You deserve to be loved and respected and it sounds like he wasn't those things for you. I admire your strength in coming out of it smart and stronger and wiser. You are certainly no piece of shit, but a beautiful and free woman from what I can gather.

That was eye opening. It speaks to how we need to follow our instincts. Some of us have a voice in our head screaming, "Danger, Danger!" and others have this faint little whisper, "Something isn't right here." Years of therapy helped me to tune into that little whispering voice. I wrote back to her.

Hey, I'm just happy that you didn't get into a relationship with him like I did. At the time I wanted to reach out and warn you, but I was also pretty young and just didn't know what to do or say. Stephen was so charismatic, that no one believed me when I said he was abusive.

She replied.

And that's exactly how my abusive ex was. So charming and charismatic to others, always everyone's favorite guy. As soon as we were behind doors and he got slightly upset or annoyed, boom, personality switch. I completely know how they can be.

Never in a million years did I expect to find common ground with Denise. "Thanks again for chatting. I know this was probably awkward!"

From there we talked about keeping in touch and ended the conversation.

Ever since I began to talk about the abuse I suffered, I'm amazed how many women confide in me about their own experience with abuse. So many are affected but never talk about it until someone else tells them they have experienced the same things. I don't know if this was the case with Denise, but so much abuse happens and goes unreported or unspoken. I get it; reporting doesn't work for most of us.

"Do you have proof?"

"Where are the pictures of your black eye?"

"Where are the X-rays of your broken bones?"

Some of us don't have those. I never had a broken bone and I never had bruises that were visible to others, and I never thought to take pictures of my bruised legs, hips, or sides. But this doesn't mean we are not abused. Abuse comes in so many different forms. For me the emotional abuse was so much more damaging than the physical assaults. I am all healed from my physical bruises, but the emotional wounds plague me today.

I didn't even know that emotional abuse was a thing until I went into therapy. I thought domestic abuse was when a woman was hit. What I knew was what I saw in Lifetime movies: the woman gets thrown down the stairs and wears layers of concealer to cover up the wounds. No one told me about the other stuff. I wasn't prepared for years of psychological torture. I wasn't prepared for the systematic breakdown of my self-esteem. I never knew about spousal rape either. It happened to me. After my conversation with Denise, the memories I had locked away came back in vivid detail, like a scary movie. It was a year before we separated. By that time, we were rarely intimate, maybe three times a year. Stephen was never romantic. He always had me turn away from him, no kissing, no eye contact; I could have been anyone. One night I came to bed exhausted after finishing a paper for school. He was already sleeping, but when I got into bed, he woke up and tried to have sex with me. I said no, but he kept trying. I said no again. He flipped me over onto my back and forced himself on me. It didn't matter how hard I was pushing him away and how many times I said no. It was physically painful and emotionally devastating. I had no agency over my own body. I had no choice. Even when you are married, no means no.

As people began returning my emails and phone calls, I realized with each person I spoke to, more memories might reveal themselves. Was I ready for what might come next? Did I want to live through this again? I wasn't sure, but I knew I needed to continue.

TWELVE

The Coworker

My conversation with Denise gave me the courage to continue with my "interviews." Already I was getting a clearer picture of my time with Stephen and who he was. Memories were coming back to me every day, and some days it was overwhelming, but now that I had started my investigation of my own life, I couldn't turn back.

When I spoke to Nick about his article, he mentioned James Nichols. James contacted him after reading the article on LinkedIn and basically set him straight about Stephen. I wasn't ready to take things any further, but Nick had offered to make an introduction to James. As I started my investigation, which turned into writing this book, I decided it was time for me to throw caution to the wind.

I spent all day psyching myself up to talk to James. In my head I kept playing out all of the possible outcomes. Will he be mean to me? Will he agree to give me information? Does he know who I am, and if not, when I tell him will he be upset? Will I like what I hear from him?

I messaged Nick. "Hey, I would be interested in talking to James Nichols. Could you introduce us?"

Within a few minutes I got a new message from Nick with James copied. "Hello James, I would like to offer an intro to Sarah. I shared that you had been kind enough to provide some information about Stephen and she's asked me to connect the two of you. Thank you so much, I will let you both speak further from here."

That was fast. I wanted to talk to him, but now I felt my stomach fluttering nervously. Ten minutes later I got a response: "Hi Sarah! Here's my number. I can talk usually at night and on weekends if that's OK."

I replied: "That's great! I'm available most nights and weekends. Does one night this week work for you?"

"Sure! Tomorrow night is good. Looking forward to it."

The next day, I sent him a text to set up a time to talk on the phone.

I spent most of the day making a list of all the things I wanted to ask him about and anxiously awaiting our phone call. Once the designated time arrived, I cautiously picked up the phone and dialed.

He was pleasant as we made our introductions. I cut to the chase and let him know why I was asking him these questions. I decided sharing that I was investigating my own life to fill in the missing pieces would sound strange, so I took the leap and mentioned the book.

"I'm writing a book about my experiences with Stephen," I told him. "I'm looking to talk to other people who knew him in order to get a well-rounded view of him. I don't want the book to come off as biased because of my experiences."

He told me that he understood and he would start from the beginning, when he met Stephen.

> I met Stephen in 2012 when I took a break from my consulting business to teach bass part time at the Musician Central where Stephen was the general manager. I have a background in IT securities and social engineering. I had done well for myself and my wife financially, but I was exhausted with all the hours I was working, so I decided to take a break and just do something I loved for a while. Stephen quickly saw in me things that he wanted and wanted to be. I was big into fitness, especially CrossFit and mountain biking and I had a really nice expensive bass that I used for the teaching gig. Everyone in the store drooled over it.

I thought of the image Stephen always tried to put forward while we were married. He wanted people to believe that he had lots of money, was the best guitar player and musician, was into fine Scotches, and was very health and fitness oriented. From what James was telling me, and from his picture on LinkedIn, I could see that he was financially set, physically fit and attractive. He was someone Stephen would have admired.

He went on. "Stephen quickly befriended me and I started to offer little mentorship moments to him. I noticed that he didn't handle his employee issues well."

This comment gave me flashbacks to when Stephen was the general manager at a Massachusetts location of Musician Central. He had a few new hires but never mailed their paperwork to corporate. He tried to blame it on one of his employees by saying he was trying to mentor him to become a manager and the guy dropped the ball. That's when Stephen was demoted to a sales rep and we moved back to Florida. James related a story to me about an incident when he tried to mentor Stephen.

> I saw some stuff going down with an employee so I approached him and asked if he would be interested in some advice. Stephen responded with a

backhanded compliment "Yeah, man, I mean, you're a big important consultant guy, tell me what to do." I noticed the backhandedness right away but decided to ignore it for the sake of the other employee. Stephen and I went into his office, and I advised him on how to manage the situation. Later it got back to the employee that I had stepped in to guide the situation, so the employee came over and thanked me for helping. I made a comment to the employee to the effect that "Stephen is a good guy and is just maybe young and needed guidance." The employee replied with "Yeah I'm not so sure he is a good guy."

At this point I was still not 100 percent sure where James stood with his opinion of Stephen. I could tell that he had some reservations about his character, but he was still friends with him for a while. I decided that I wouldn't say too much about my opinion. I mostly kept quiet and just interjected an "mmm hmm" or another form of acknowledgment to show I heard what he said. I wasn't sure if James knew Stephen during the time of our marriage until the next story he told me.

So back then I worked out a lot. Stephen always wanted to talk to me about fitness and get tips and advice. I told him I could help him get in better shape. Stephen kept saying he was trying to look like Chris Hemsworth from *Thor*. Stephen said they already looked alike, as they are both blond, tall, and have broad shoulders. I mean, I didn't want to hurt his feelings, so I never said anything. Stephen was strong but he wasn't in shape, so he would always try to bull his way through based off brute strength. Stephen and I started mountain biking together. Everything we did for fitness Stephen would hurt himself. This one time when we were mountain biking Stephen fell and busted his leg pretty badly.

This caused a flash in my mind. "Wait, was this to his right shin?" I asked.

"Yeah, I think so," he replied.

"OK, I remember that. He came home and was all bloody and his leg was messed up. I remember cleaning the wound for him as he refused to go to the ER. I had to bandage it up."

"So you knew Stephen when he and I were still married?" I asked him flat-out.

"Yes, I did. I remember him talking about you a little bit, but I never met you."

OK, so he knew I existed. I wondered what Stephen's excuse was for the divorce. What did he tell people?

James talked about their doing CrossFit together. "Stephen again would try and do things based on pure strength but no technique and tried to advance too quickly. He never wanted to work on the skills needed to do things correctly so he could avoid injury. He wanted to be the strongest guy there but didn't have technique. Basically, he wanted to show off. This led to him tearing his ACL."

I mentioned Denise to James. I heard him take a breath and he kind of sighed, "Yeah...." I sensed he knew where I was going, so I went ahead and pushed through.

"I suspected an inappropriate relationship between the two of them," I said.

"Yes, I saw that too," he interjected. "I pulled Stephen aside and spoke to him about it. I told him that it wasn't right. He was having a relationship with this woman, and he was her boss and he was married, so I told him he should stop it."

"Well," I replied, "she would call him at two in the morning, and he would go outside our apartment to talk to her. If I asked him who called, he would say it was the store. When I pressed the issue on why he was outside and not just in the other room, he acted like it made perfect sense, that he just didn't want to wake me."

I recognized now that this is classic gaslighting. The store was calling at 2 a.m. and he was being considerate by taking the call outside. I was unnecessarily suspicious and "not well." Abusers twist things around to make you feel like you are the crazy one, not them.

"Oh, wow." I could hear the shock and sympathy in his voice. I could tell already that James was a devoted husband and father who was strong in his faith.

I told him that I reached out to Denise to get her side of the story and he sounded surprised but interested in what she had to say.

"Denise told me that on her side, she and Stephen were just really close friends. She admitted feeling some guilt that she should never have been that close to a married man, but that she hadn't had intentions for things to go any further than that. She did say that she isn't sure that Stephen had the same intentions."

"I can definitely see that being true based on what I observed. I don't think there's any reason not to believe her," James reflected.

I went on. "She also shared with me that Stephen's behavior changed when she started dating someone during their friendship. She told me that her boyfriend would see Stephen driving by his house multiple times a week."

"What?" James sounded shocked.

"Yeah, I mean, Stephen drove a fairly distinct green Jeep and the boyfriend knew Stephen and he knew the Jeep."

"Well, Stephen really did have some OCD or obsessive tendencies, so I guess that makes sense," he agreed.

"James, I've always had questions about the cancer situation."

"OK, I might be able to answer some questions about that but not much. Mostly timeline questions because he really did disappear."

"Well, here is what I know," I started. I shared the story of hearing about Stephen's cancer and calling his mother. I finished with an inward grimace. "So basically, James, I told his mother he had cancer."

James sighed and muttered an inaudible phrase indicating disbelief. James then told me what he knew.

"Stephen was sick," he paused. "What exactly he was sick with I don't know. He and I lost contact after I left Musician Central, when I decided to start up a new business. I tried to contact him for four months and he wouldn't return my calls or text messages. I reached out to a guy from Musician Central asking if they had heard from Stephen and they were like 'No, man, we haven't heard from him since he was fired.' 'He was fired?' I was kind of surprised. And the guy said, 'Yeah, man, there was something wrong with the inventory paperwork or something and they fired him.'"

After James related this conversation to me, I interrupted. "James, I can clear this detail up for you."

"Really? How do you know what happened?"

"The same woman who called to tell me about the cancer told me. She spoke to Miguel Martinez," I said.

"Hmm, I recognize that name. Is he a Musician Central guy?" James asked.

"He is. What happened is ... Stephen stole a guitar for a woman he was dating."

James interrupted, putting the pieces together. "I know that woman. I remember Stephen dated someone who was a musician!"

"Yes, exactly," I confirmed, "he dated her prior to Angela. Well, when they broke up Stephen tried to return the guitar to the store by sneaking it in and entering it back into inventory. He was caught and then fired for theft."

"Wow, that makes sense." James sighed, sounding like he just had an epiphany. We got back to the story James was telling me.

James continued. "Eventually Stephen reached out to me by sending a text that said 'Hey, man! Where have you been?' and I replied to him, 'What do you mean, where have I been? I've been texting you for four months and you haven't replied.' Stephen texted back acting like I was crazy, and then he said maybe his phone was messed up. He made all sorts of excuses, but he wouldn't admit that he was just too embarrassed that he was fired to face me for four months. I decided to drop it and we made plans to get coffee. At coffee we talked about how he was now living with Dr. Perelman, helping him start up his new practice. From there we picked up on our friendship where we had left off."

I wondered to myself how James could have reestablished the friendship. But I remembered how charming Stephen could be. He might have twisted the story of the theft in a way that made James comfortable. I couldn't judge. I stayed married to the man for six years.

"Stephen reached out to me to get assistance with setting up the IT portion of Doc's new business," James told me. "This is my area of expertise, and I was happy to help since I knew both of them from Musician Central. Doc and I became friends. I had started up a business before and was starting another one, so Doc and I had a lot of conversations about that. He told me that Stephen's salary was $50,000, and he had Stephen scheduling appointments and doing a lot of office work. Stephen told me that he was bored with it and didn't want to be doing that kind of work. I told him that he had it pretty good. He was making decent money, more than he had been at Musician Central, and he was on the ground floor of a budding new practice. I told him that if he put in the grunt work now it would pay off later. Stephen didn't really want to hear it. He wanted instant gratification."

This resonated with me. "I can see that being true. Stephen always wanted people to believe we had a lot of money, but ironically, we could have been more comfortable financially if he had curbed his spending. He didn't want to save money now to be set up for later; he wanted that high life now and didn't want to work for it."

"Well," James replied, "Stephen kept talking to me about wanting to do consulting like I did. So I brought him into my business parttime and tried to train him. To get him started, I gave him some training modules (e-learning videos) and some homework. Stephen didn't pay attention to the modules and didn't do the homework. It wasn't long before I told him that it wasn't the right time for us to work together, as Stephen didn't seem to be into it. My impression was that Stephen wasn't interested in working; he just wanted to be the boss and have others do the work."

I thought to myself that what Stephen wanted was the title. He wanted to tell people, "I'm a consultant." He wanted the lifestyle, not the actual job. James was giving me more to think about.

He went on. "He called me to help with network issues with Doc's business. Stephen would always tell me that Doc was doing business on all these international sites. He believed that was the reason the network was bogging down. I would go in to provide some cleanup and ultimately found that Stephen had tried to clear his browsing history but hadn't done a good enough job. I found evidence of porn and gun buying websites on the company computers. I cleaned it all out and told Stephen to stop looking at this stuff, especially at work. I honestly didn't care what he looked at, but I didn't want to be exposed to it every time I helped with the computers."

I thought back to when Stephen put passwords on the phone and the laptop. At the time I thought it was about hiding his relationship with Denise. Now I wondered about all those nights he was in the bedroom while I did my homework. Maybe he was doing more than playing video games. Maybe he was surfing porn.

James recalled, "I noticed Stephen purchasing a lot of guns. We went out to a local gun range. It had five bays. Stephen gets there and takes up all five bays setting up a different gun in each bay. It was very showy and just really bad gun range etiquette. It was embarrassing. One of the guns he had was this really nice rifle. I remember it distinctly because I was jealous! I really wanted that gun. I asked him about it because I knew he couldn't afford it. I was like 'Stephen, where did you get this? With the way you have it set up this is like a $3,500 gun!' 'It was $4,000 actually.' I asked him, 'Did you buy this?' and he said, 'Well, my dad and I buy guns all the time. We like to collect them.' I was confused so I pressed him. 'So did your dad buy it or did you buy it?' 'I bought it,' Stephen finally admitted."

James went on for a little longer about how many rare and expensive guns Stephen had purchased and collected. He talked about Stephen boasting about going shooting with his dad all the time. I got the feeling from James that he knew something wasn't right with Stephen and Doc, but not having any proof other than thinking his spending habits were not in proportion with his salary, he couldn't really do anything about it.

He continued, "Stephen told me that he was making $80,000 a year, but I remembered that Doc had told me a lesser number. I decided to ask Doc about it; for all I knew he had given Stephen a raise. When I asked Doc about this he said, 'I pay him $50,000. I don't know why he would say $80,000. I guess maybe he wants to seem cool. He's just weird.'"

I found it interesting that Doc had some inclination that Stephen was off but not enough to raise any red flags. This seemed to be a pattern with people around Stephen, including myself. That tiny voice whispering, "This doesn't make sense" was so often ignored when Stephen was spinning his distortions and lies.

James expanded on Stephen's weirdness. "Doc had this boat; it was a $350,000 Boston Whaler that Doc had purchased as a treat to himself after having just gone through a tough divorce. He would allow Stephen to use it whenever he wanted to. We went out one day and Stephen pulled up next to a group of guys who also had a nice boat. The guys were looking at the Whaler and complimenting it. Stephen started telling them all about the boat and the features of it, acting like he owned it. I thought this was weird that Stephen never said this was his friend's boat. I really wanted to make a comment like 'Oh yeah, Doc loves his boat.' But I didn't ... though now I kinda wish I had."

Stephen's "lie by omission" about the boat reminded me of things he did when we were married. He was all about the outward appearance of wealth and success. But I also realized that people in his orbit often covered for him. James didn't call out his lie about the boat. I never told anyone what was happening behind closed doors.

"Stephen was always like that," I told him. "He would buy $100 jeans, but our electricity would get shut off, and we hadn't had cable for two years because he wanted to eat fancy dinners and buy expensive shoes rather than use the money to pay our bills."

James found this shocking. He let out a sigh and a little gasp of disbelief. I could only imagine him thinking about his own wife and child, as I told him that on more than one occasion, I got home from work and tried to use the garage door opener, only to find it dead because Stephen failed to pay the electric bill again.

"Well, I can tell you that Stephen loved to use the boat but never wanted to clean it after. All he needed to do was take out the trash we made while out there, and spray it down with the water hose, didn't take longer than 15 to 20 minutes, but he wouldn't do it."

I was getting flashbacks about the mess at our house. Most nights, Stephen ate his dinner in bed, where I was required to serve his food like a maid. After eating, he left his dirty plates and silverware by the bed. He left Coke cans wherever he finished them. We could never have friends over without at least a three-day warning so that I could clean like a madwoman. When he wanted to be angry about something, he would berate me because the house was so disgusting and I should be a better housekeeper. I was always overwhelmed and frustrated and felt so worthless. I was nothing but a glorified servant to him.

I wanted to know more about Angela, Stephen's girlfriend at the time of his death. I had no clue about their relationship. I only had his mother's version, which was that he died of a broken heart and that Angela was a gold digger only out for money, so when I spoke to James and got his take on the whole relationship, I was shocked.

"Yeah, I knew Angela, but not well. I mostly knew what Stephen told me about her and their relationship. Stephen would come to me for relationship advice. Angela's parents never liked Stephen and tried to get her away from him. They moved her back to Colorado in an attempt to do that. Stephen talked all the time about wanting to marry Angela. I tried to counsel him on what to do about it because Angela was hesitant. I told him to back off, that Angela wasn't ready and he needed to respect that. I advised if he really wanted to marry her, he needed to get along with her parents. Stephen got exasperated and said he was trying, but her family just didn't get his jokes."

This almost made me laugh. His jokes. Of course, his jokes were not funny; they were just cruel. I thought back to his always trying to frighten me, and later, the YouTube video of Stephen's memorial service of his brother telling the "funny" story that was actually thoughtless and mean. I made a note to ask James if he attended the funeral before we get off the phone.

James continued, "Stephen spent a fortune on dinners when Angela came to town. Angela would always tell him that they didn't need to do that. She suggested staying home or someplace cheaper, but Stephen wouldn't listen."

This didn't sound like the woman his mother described to me. Carol made it sound like Angela was forcing him to spend all this money on her. It sounded to me like he was spending all this money to trap her. I thought back to all the dinners out Stephen and I had when we were dating.

Then James said, "Stephen would also spend a fortune on flights to Colorado to visit Angela after she moved. Well, Angela didn't want him coming to visit her that often. She was trying to get space from him, but he wouldn't let her ... he kept going out there. After Stephen was arrested, Angela visited him in jail a few times and eventually made the difficult decision that she needed to separate herself from him. She let him know this was happening and then stopped responding to phone calls and text messages."

"Who could blame her?" I interjected.

"I did the same thing, actually," James said. "I received a text message from Stephen, 'Doc is framing me! I didn't do this!' Because of the nature of my work, I just felt that I needed to distance myself from him and the whole situation. I sent Stephen a text that said, 'Man, I can't be involved. I am still your friend, and I am praying for you.' After the suicide Angela reached out to me and the two of us talked about how we each had some guilt. Maybe we contributed to Stephen's suicide. We felt that if we hadn't abandoned him maybe he wouldn't have felt alone and wouldn't have killed himself."

At this point I needed to interject. "James, I've done a lot of research on mental health issues related to my life with Stephen. I believe that he had an antisocial personality disorder; more specifically, I believe he was a sociopath."

I felt nervous sharing this with James. I wasn't sure how he would react. It was a strong opinion on Stephen's mental state. But he replied without hesitation.

"I one hundred percent agree."

I went on to say, "I've done some research on sociopathy and it does tend to be shocking when sociopaths die by suicide because they are so narcissistic. I know that I was shocked because there was no one in this world that Stephen loved more than himself. I never thought he would hurt himself, only others. However, what I found is that when the mask is off, and there are no other options to hide, they can no longer talk their way out and they sometimes resort to suicide. It's either a way to avoid the consequences of their actions or a last-ditch effort to prove to everyone that you can't catch them, you can't hold them accountable. Only the sociopathic individual has control over their destiny. Kind of the last fuck you."

James seemed almost freed by this information. He said he never thought of it that way. I only hope that it removed some of the guilt he felt. If not, Stephen had succeeded in one last manipulation. He had others believing it was their fault he killed himself.

It had been an emotional conversation. I thanked him for talking to me and he said he would be happy to speak with me any time and answer any other questions that I might have. He had been so forthright and honest with me, I wanted to clear some things up for him. Some of the things that Stephen had shared with him were complete lies.

"I'm not sure any of this makes a difference, but I would like to offer you some insights around things you told me. Stephen was not that close with his father, and they did not go out shooting all the time. I know they went one time because they had photos on Facebook, but I'm not aware of them ever going again."

How much should I share? Why was this compulsion to cover for Stephen still within me? I decided to continue.

"Stephen was not close with his family at all. In fact, he hated his brother."

I was always so disgusted with the terrible things Stephen said about his brother. I just couldn't understand how anyone could say things like that about a family member.

James said, "Stephen mentioned to me that you sang opera."

It was a statement but also a question.

"I did when I met him. I was in college studying voice. When we first started dating, he seemed so supportive of my music. But I think he quickly became aware of the fact that I was a better musician than he was and that was a problem. So Stephen made sure to squash that right away."

James agreed with me. He said he heard Stephen play guitar at the store.

"Yeah, Stephen played guitar for me one time and I was like 'Dude, you're not playing guitar.' Stephen said, 'Oh, my hand is tired today, but I played with a band, and we toured all over the country.' I was like, 'OK, but Stephen, what you're doing here isn't playing guitar.'"

I started laughing. "Stephen never played in a band and certainly never toured the country playing with anyone. The only things he knew how to play were little licks on demo guitars. It was only impressive to people who couldn't play guitar."

James said he picked up on that right away. "I can see that. And who lies about playing in a band that toured the country? I mean, that is such an easy lie to catch with a simple Google search!"

The phone call was nearing an end, so I decided to ask him about the memorial service.

"Stephen's parents wanted me to go to his memorial service but I just couldn't go. I didn't feel like I could fly down there and pretend to laugh and talk about all the good times with Stephen when I didn't have any. Did you go?" I asked.

"No, I couldn't go for pretty much the same reasons. I didn't think he was a good person and I wanted his family to be surrounded by people who did. I wanted them to have the memorial service they wanted," James sighed.

I thought again of the memorial service video his family had posted on YouTube and seeing all of those empty seats. It had always lingered with me that maybe I should have gone anyway, if just for his parents. Hearing James outline the same reasons I had for not going to the memorial, I finally felt some peace about my decision to stay away. It also made me wonder how many of Stephen's so-called friends felt the same way. Is that why there were so many empty seats? Did everyone know who he truly was?

Thirteen

The Doctor

You have probably picked up by this time that there is another person that is integral to this story. He has been mostly referred to by people who knew Stephen as "Doc." This is the man Stephen moved in with, worked for, and ultimately stole from. He was a musician and bought a lot of stuff from Stephen at Musician Central. Through this connection they became friends. I needed to try and talk to him because by all accounts this man would have a lot to say about Stephen and was most connected to him in the time leading up to his death. I didn't have any contact information for him, so using the mailing address from the police reports I sent him the following letter.

Dr. Jacob Perelman,

You don't know me, but I am Stephen Jones's former wife. I started a journey which included writing a memoir of my time as his wife and it has led me to try and understand the events leading up to his suicide. His family has fed me a lot of different accounts of why they think it happened and none of them feel like the truth. During my research I did a Google search when trying to find an obituary. I did not find one, but I did find his mugshot. This led me to request police reports and investigation notes of his crimes against you from the Sheriff Department.

There are many parallels between your story and mine. I left Stephen in January 2012 after he attacked me. Stephen was very abusive to me both emotionally and physically over the years. After I left him, I found that he had used my information to finance tens of thousands of dollars of credit cards and store credit in my name. He lied to me and told me things were gifts or that his work had provided electronics to him. He was the only one who had a key to our mailbox and intercepted the bills. I never saw a thing. Unfortunately for me, no one believed me. The authorities couldn't do anything for me. I have been making settlements with debt collectors for over four years. I still struggle to keep my credit scores in an acceptable range.

I certainly don't want to drudge up any painful memories for you but I have some questions if you would be willing to chat with me. I understand by talking to some former friends of his that he lived with you for some time. I have listed my contact information below both phone and email. Whichever form of contact is more comfortable for you is fine with me. I hate the fact that Stephen claimed another victim and I hope that you have managed to recover both emotionally and fiscally.

Best Regards,
Sarah

On Easter weekend 2019, Dr. Perelman responded to my letter via email, advising that he would love to speak with me. But he needed to speak with his attorney first, as he was still looking into his options for restitution from Stephen's estate.

In May he told me he would talk to me. We made arrangements via email to talk on a Wednesday night. I would be the one to call. I found a quiet space in the house free from distraction. My boyfriend (now my loving husband) waited nervously in the next room. My hopes were high that I was about to get some additional answers, answers to questions that no one but the doctor could know. I wondered if he knew Stephen while we were married. The phone rang once and then a man answered. His voice sounded a little raspy but very confident; it was the voice of someone used to being in control.

"Hello, Sarah."

I put on my most pleasant-sounding voice to try and make him feel at ease talking to me and to make sure he knew that I was a friend, not a foe.

"Hi, Jacob! Thanks so much for agreeing to talk to me."

The conversation quickly became a blurring whirl.

"I've been looking for you for a long time and trying to talk to you about this guy. Let me just tell you my story."

I wondered what he meant. Why was he looking for me? But he seemed anxious to talk and I didn't want to slow him down with questions. "Sounds good. Please tell me whatever you want. If there are any questions that I can answer for you I'm happy to do that."

"I'm a plastic surgeon and I had a practice in Lake City. I am also a musician on the side and that's how I met Stephen; I was a customer of his at Musician Central. You and he had just moved back from up North, I remember."

So the doctor and I overlapped as well. I found it interesting that Stephen had never mentioned either Dr. Perelman or James. I realized that even then, less than two years into our marriage, we were already so distant. I remembered that he never asked me about school or work, but I never asked him about anything either. Actually, I was afraid to ask him anything. I never knew when an attempt at normal conversation would trigger his rage.

He continued, "Well, Stephen got transferred to another location down south and my surgical practice was blowing up so I took that opportunity and moved down to that area as well. Stephen seemed like a good guy but quirky. Then all of a sudden Stephen disappeared from Musician Central. I finally found him. He had quit Musician Central and was living in a small apartment on University. I told him that I wanted to start my own practice and brought him on to help me. I let him move in with me at this time. Things seemed fine, but one day his Jeep was missing and apparently your dad had it impounded, and I gave him the $5,000 to get the Jeep out of impound."

"That never happened," I interjected.

"What do you mean?" He sounded shocked.

"My father never had his Jeep impounded. Anyone who knows my father knows that he would never do that," I explained.

"Great. Another one of Stephen's lies uncovered." He was angry, and rightfully so.

"Also, he didn't quit Musician Central; he was fired for stealing a guitar for a girlfriend," I told him, wanting to clarify his comment about Stephen "quitting" his job.

"Yes, I know he was fired for stealing and actually stole a lot of things from them," he said. He switched gears and began to tell me that he had tried to find me before Stephen died. "You know, I tried to find you before. My attorney and I hired a private investigator to track you down."

A private investigator? I was a little put off by this. It struck me as creepy, but then I realized I was the one currently investigating my own life, tracking down people to interview. It might have been funny, but I thought about Stephen's chaos leaving all of us looking for answers. Like victims of a preventable disaster, we were all looking for clues.

"I never updated my address. I didn't want Stephen to find me and I guess it worked."

"Yeah, it did, so then we tried to find you through your dad. Are you still in Bath?"

I was a bit surprised as I hadn't said anything about what city I lived in or where I worked. "No, I don't live in Bath anymore."

"Is your dad still at the shipyard?" he asked.

He wasn't aggressive towards me when asking these questions, but I got the feeling he really wanted me to know that he wasn't lying and had done his research on me. I had a sudden brief worry that maybe he was looking for me because he thought I was involved in Stephen's crimes.

"No, actually he is retired now and traveling. I no longer work for BIW either, but I still work for the Navy." I volunteered some additional information, hoping to show him that I believed him and I didn't think of him as a threat. He began sharing more details.

"Stephen was always dating women. Even when he had a girlfriend, he was still on the online dating apps talking to other girls. Kristen was his first girlfriend after you two, and her friends kept telling her she needed to break up with him because they got really bad vibes from the guy."

"Oh, I think she is the girl he stole the guitar for," I responded. I wondered about Kristen. Had he been seeing her the year we got divorced? Not that I cared what he was doing that year, but maybe she was the reason he didn't show up at court. He had moved on by then. My mind snapped back to the present. Suddenly Dr. Perelman was nearly yelling into the phone.

"He robbed me! I gave the guy the keys to my life, and he robbed me!"

He took a deep breath. "He was dating that Angela girl and went up to visit her. I found some things that looked off. My mom was here visiting me, and we started digging around. I looked in Stephen's car and found more evidence of what he was doing, and I called the police. I have connections to law enforcement in this area, so when I called them, they knew to take it seriously. The guy bought firearms and fancy dinners and took trips to Europe with my money! The guy was so terrible. I'm Jewish, and he even tried to tell me some crap about going to Jerusalem with a family member to get money."

"You know that was a lie as well; the grandfather that he said was dead wasn't and actually just died not this past Christmas but the one before," I clarified.

"Oh, yeah, I know," he snapped back.

I interjected at this time and told him that I was able to obtain copies of the police reports, partly because I didn't want him to relive all of this unless he wanted to and partly because I wanted more information than what was on the police reports.

"How did you find out about this?" he asked me.

"Well, his parents called me right after the police left their house. Literally within 30 minutes of his death they called me. So they didn't have much information. All they said was his body was found in the woods and it was a homicide or a suicide and they were waiting for the police."

At that point Jacob jumped in and said, "Yeah, the guy went out to a park, sat on a park bench and ate a bullet."

I could hear the anger and contempt in his voice, but I was still a little shocked. It was such a crude thing to say. But he had been betrayed by someone he trusted, and his anger was still fresh.

"Yes, I know," I told him. "I was able to get copies of those police reports as well. Over the next couple days his parents were so hard to get information from and I wanted to know what was going on, so I put his name into a Google search hoping to find an obituary or a news article talking about a murder or something to give me answers. Instead, I found his mugshot. I was able to see what the charges were, but I didn't know the details behind them until about a year later. His parents have never told me the truth about what happened."

Jacob jumped in again. "His family is disgusting. They are all crazy and liars. They have been on a smear campaign against me since this whole thing went down. They told everyone that I'm a liar and that Stephen didn't do any of this stuff."

"I believe you!" I said emphatically. "How can anyone deny it? He admitted on the phone with you that was being recorded by police." I wanted him to know I really had read the police reports and I knew he was telling the truth.

"I asked his parents for my stuff back and they acted like I was a terrible person. They said, 'How can you ask us that? Our son is dead and these are his things!' I told them no, they aren't his things; he bought them with my money. They are mine. That guy had almost $5,000 in firearms and things that he bought with my money, which, by the way, is a first degree felony! He could get life in prison for buying firearms during the commission of a crime."

This was new information to me. I knew that he bought the guns with stolen money, but I didn't know that it would be a bigger crime to buy weapons while committing a felony.

"His family is messed up. My investigator looked into his parents, and they found some weird things in Roger's past. There was something about an arrest at an anti-abortion protest when he was younger." He told me as kind of a warning to watch out for Stephen's family.

"That doesn't surprise me. They are very conservative and religious. Honestly, though, I always felt they were good people, until I started writing this book. Looking back and writing my story has brought up memories about them. I remember crying in the back seat of their car, asking them why their son was so mean and looking for advice on how to deal with him. His mother looked back at me and said, 'It's the woman's lot in life to suffer.' I mean, who says that to a girl who is crying and obviously being abused?"

I thought back to that day in the car. I was still trying to understand Stephen at that time, thinking if I just had the right formula, the magic words, the sweet man I had dated would come back. His parents had to have the key. I thought of them as my lifeline. But they shut me down. It wasn't just my fault that Stephen was angry all the time; it was my lot in life. That conversation was one of many that I locked away from myself. I was so confused and hurt. I felt betrayed by people I relied on and trusted. It wasn't a comfortable memory.

"They are all sick people," Jacob replied. He asked me about my experience with Stephen.

"We have kind of a similar situation, Jacob. He started stealing from me within the first two months of our marriage. He got promoted and told me that all new managers got a laptop. But really, he used my information to finance it online."

Jacob interjected, "He bought a laptop with my money too. He practiced all this on you before he did it to me."

"Pretty much. When I left him, I needed to buy a new car. That's when I found my credit destroyed and all this debt. He had the only mailbox key at every apartment we lived at and hid the bills from me, just like he did to you," I told him.

"Well, I hope you were able to recover and get over this. I hope you can move on," he said.

"Oh, I moved on. I'm just tired of other people telling my story and lying about Stephen," I responded. "Honestly, I was scared to reach out to you. I didn't know if you would be angry with me because I didn't do more to get Stephen in trouble during our divorce. But at that time, I just needed to get away from him. No one would believe that he could steal from me; they felt that, as his wife, I should have known everything he was doing to me."

"I get it. He totally duped me, and I wasn't smart enough to see it," he said.

"Not at all; that's not how I see it. We're both smart, educated people. But we're also kind. You opened up your home to a friend in need and he screwed you. Neither of us are criminals so we don't think like criminals. We got tangled up with someone who in my opinion was a sociopath and he took advantage of our kindness."

I continued, "Stephen left me with nothing. He was very abusive throughout our entire marriage, and I just couldn't see a way out until Denise Olsen. Did you know her?"

"Yup, I remember her. Stephen talked to her for a long time. Even while he was dating Kristen. He was always talking to multiple women," he answered.

"Well, I'm grateful I found him talking to her, because that let me know that he didn't really care about me all that much. If I left, he would have someone else to focus on. So we agreed to get divorced and it seemed amicable at first but one day he came home...."

"And he assaulted you, didn't he?!"

"Yes, he did," I confirmed. I told him about the night I left. "I was homeless. I lived in my car for around two weeks because he cleaned out the bank accounts as soon as I left. Oh, and he had the audacity to call me when my first paycheck went into my new bank account and ask me where the money was. I told him I had my checks moved to my own bank account and he said, 'Well, how the hell am I supposed to eat?!'"

"He actually asked you how he was supposed to eat?" Jacob was half laughing in disbelief. "That guy was a monster. I always suspected that he assaulted you, but I was never able to confirm it. What he did to me is terrible, but you never hit a woman. I really hope that you are OK and that you can move on and find happiness and a better life."

"Oh, I have," I assured him. "I'm actually very happy. I didn't do it alone, though. I went to therapy, and I have a cousin in the mental health field who helped me deal with it. I'm in a great relationship now with a truly kind man. Also, I gained a ton of weight while married to Stephen and was obese when I left him. I've lost 115 pounds, so I'm now happy and healthy."

"Good for you!" he said.

"Honestly, I feel bad for you because you didn't get closure. You couldn't go to court and you didn't get restitution from him," I said.

"Don't you worry about me getting closure. I have all the closure I need. As far as I am concerned, I put the bullet in his head," he nearly growled.

I was a little taken aback by this statement. It was harsh but understandable based on what Stephen put this man through. He must have realized what he said, because he began to clarify.

"Don't get me wrong; I didn't murder Stephen, but I turned him in. I showed everyone what he is and he decided he couldn't live with that."

"My cousin actually works in suicide prevention, so we've had some conversations about this. Stephen was never evaluated by a mental health professional, but our armchair diagnosis of him is that he was a sociopath. Sociopaths will typically end their lives by suicide for one of two reasons. First, they see no way out. The mask has been removed and they are backed into a corner, for example, facing prison time. So instead of letting you get them, they take their own life as a way to stay in control of their destiny. Second, it's their last chance to victimize people. There's no way out, and instead of facing the music, they decide to end their life by suicide. They often leave a suicide note to make others feel bad or guilty, like it was their fault. But there wasn't a suicide note from Stephen so it may have been the former," I explained to him.

"There was a suicide note," he said.

"What? Really?" After all of my research and conversations with Stephen's parents, I had never heard this. I was surprised and felt my understanding of everything start to shift.

"Yes, he sent a note to Angela. She read it to me. It said he was in love with her and stuff about them not being together. It doesn't outright blame her, though."

"OK, well, this makes sense as to why his parents told me he died of a broken heart and why they blame Angela." I was stunned. I knew enough about Stephen's methods that I understood he was, indeed, blaming her. What a cruel thing to do.

"Stephen was obsessed with Angela," Jacob continued. "I mean, the guy bought her an engagement ring with my money from a diamond broker that I set him up with! Of course, he was cheating on her this whole time too."

"That's just scummy." I thought of the layers to Stephen's betrayals. They didn't end. "I actually reached out to her on Facebook asking if she would talk to me," I told him.

"Be careful with her." He paused as if considering his next words. "She's pretty crazy herself. You're strong and she just isn't. She needed to get counseling but never did. She's very unstable and she still talks to his parents. Stephen didn't have to die. All I needed from him was the truth. I needed him to tell the truth about what he did and how he did it so that I could sue the bank that let him access my safety deposit box. He stole $250,000 from me. I wasn't getting that back from him. I mean, I wrote that off as a business loss, so I'm fine. But I need to sue the bank."

I hadn't thought of this. Reading the police reports, I had wondered how Jacob was going to get his money from Stephen's "estate" when I was sure that estate was in the negative. It never occurred to me he just needed evidence to sue the bank. But I guess either way, Stephen was going to jail, and that humiliation was too much for him.

Jacob went on. "When Stephen killed himself, the case was closed as unsolved due to insufficient evidence. His parents, of course, jumped all over that as proof I lied and that Stephen was innocent. You know, Stephen at one point called me and told me, 'I'm sick, OK?' insinuating that he stole from me because he couldn't help himself. I guess he thought because I'm a doctor I would have sympathy."

I found this interesting. Did Stephen really know that he was unwell? I wondered if he had the awareness that his behavior wasn't typical. Maybe he was struggling with his compulsions. I never knew Stephen to be introspective in the least. It was more likely he was being manipulative again.

"Jacob, do you mind if I ask you a very specific question about Stephen? I was told by family and friends, and later Stephen in an email, that he was diagnosed with non–Hodgkin's lymphoma."

Before I could ask if Stephen had cancer Jacob jumped in. "There was never any evidence of cancer. I asked him about it several times as I had heard the same thing and he would always tell me, 'That's personal.' He refused to talk about it."

"His parents told me that he was living with a doctor that was helping take care of him during his cancer treatments," I told him.

"I picked him up from the hospital once after he had surgery for a severely deviated septum. That's it."

You would think if you lived with a doctor, you would talk to them about your medical things, but he never would.

"Stephen told me in an email that he had paid $750,000 in experimental cancer treatments and then within a year he was cured," I told him.

"Yeah, that's not possible. I believe the cancer story was a lie to cover up drug abuse," he said.

I agreed with him. This is what I have always thought as well. The last time I saw him in person he had lost so much weight and just didn't look well.

I thanked him for speaking with me and we ended our call. I felt exhausted. While he told me not to feel bad for him, I really couldn't help it. I understood and empathized with what he went through and was still going through. If Stephen and I had stayed together, my salary would have been four times larger than his by now. He would have continued stealing from me, in greater and greater amounts. I thought back to his joke about my falling through the ice and the life insurance. I knew without a doubt now that the path he was on was a dark one. One day, watching me die would have been nothing for him if a payday was at stake.

I thought of Jacob telling his story and not having people believe him. I knew what that felt like. But on top of that, Stephen's family was waging a smear campaign against him, actively fighting against him, when he had evidence of Stephen's crimes. It was so hard for me to understand how Stephen's family could be so blind to who their son really was.

FOURTEEN

The Girlfriend

Angela Plourde was a huge part of this puzzle that I was seeking to put together. Stephen had bought her a ring and written her a suicide note. I wanted to know what her experience of him was. Which Stephen had she known? I waited a few weeks after finding her before reaching out.

I had a few concerns about contacting her. First, I was afraid of her relationship with Stephen's parents. I didn't want my conversation with her or word of my investigation to get back to them. They never told me the truth about what was going on in Stephen's life during this time. From Jacob, I gathered that they were angry about everything. They might lash out at me for asking Angela for information, and even worse, for telling the truth about my relationship with their son. Second, I didn't want to do any damage to Angela. I didn't know what her feelings were or where she was in her recovery process from this grief. After a lot of thought and mustering up the courage, I carefully crafted a Facebook message to her.

> Hi Angela, we have a shared history and I wonder if you would be willing to chat about it. We both had relationships with Stephen Jones. He and I were married for six years before divorcing in 2012. I know this might be a tough topic for you, as I have heard that you were still in a relationship with him at the time of his death. I am so sorry you have experienced this loss.
>
> I am just trying to understand a few things as I get conflicting information from his family and his friends. Would you be able to provide some clarity?
>
> Again, if this is too hard to discuss I understand ... however, based on my experience with Stephen, I also believe I may have some insights for you as well that might hopefully help you understand him more.
>
> Please let me know if you would like to talk with me or not.
> Thanks—Sarah

I nervously hit send. For the rest of the day, I looked at my phone every few minutes. Part of me was hoping that she would respond, and the other part was terrified she would. I was scared that she might be angry and threaten to call his parents. Five minutes felt like five days waiting for a reply that didn't come. I woke up the next morning and looked at my phone right away, hoping for a response. One day turned to three days and I pretty much gave up hope that she was going to message me back. By day four I stopped looking at my phone, expecting a message from her. I was disappointed and feeling like I had hit a dead end. Then, one night when I was getting into bed, my phone lit up with a new message notification. I rolled over and picked up the phone to see a new message from Angela. My heart started racing and I cautiously opened Messenger to read what she had to say.

> *Sarah, I try to remember the best about Stephen. The reason I was so side swiped when it happened was because so much was secret until the end. I experienced extreme grief and feeling betrayed at the same time. It is tragic what happened … certainly not worth losing life. What is it you need clarity on?*

I felt a myriad of emotions. It seemed like she was putting me on notice to be careful what I said about him, as she only wanted to remember the good things about him. I didn't want to say something that would upset her and make her stop talking. In my reply I wanted to validate her feelings that he didn't need to die and that this was, indeed, a sad event.

> I'm sure you were devastated when he died. I know I was very sad to hear things came to that for him. I guess I just don't understand why. I spoke to his friend James, and he told me one thing, but when this all happened his parents told me another version. I just thought since you were probably closest to him you might have a better idea as to why he would end his life by suicide.

> *His family has not accepted what happened. I love Carol and Roger, but they can't accept his actions.*

> Yeah, I have gathered that from them…

> *Even though I have accepted it, I still choose to believe he was a good person at heart. He got wrapped up in something bad. He became secluded. The devil does his best work in isolation. It could happen to any of us who does not guard our heart.*

This stunned me. "I still choose to believe he was a good person at heart." What did this mean? She knew he did terrible things, but she was choosing to ignore his actions and act like he was a good person? This made me a little angry. Even with black and white proof she voluntarily closed her eyes to the truth of who he was. In the moment, I wanted to yell at her. Later, I realized I wanted to yell at my younger self. It was like traveling in a time machine to a version of myself that still believed Stephen was a good man. A version of myself who was still putting up with his abuse because it was my fault. I wanted to shout at that younger me and warn her. Angela wasn't me, and I took a second to remember that she was also his victim. He may not have graduated to physical violence with her, but he was definitely manipulating her emotionally.

She spoke of "the devil" and I realized she was trying to make sense of this all from a religious and biblical standpoint. I was cautious with her after this because I didn't want to get into a theological debate with her. I am a Christian, but I really don't like when people throw out the quip "The devil made me do it." I've seen many instances of mental health issues in the church covered up or ignored with this statement. Stephen was not well and he needed treatment; it had nothing to do with "the devil."

He was always giving … very giving. He would spend irresponsibly which I didn't like, but we were not married so his finances weren't my business.
Yes. He was that way when we were dating as well.

Angela seemed to ignore the fact he was buying her gifts with money he stole. She was only focusing on how "giving" he was. It felt like she had compartmentalized a great deal to survive the trauma, closing off the worst parts so she could focus on the good parts.

I thought well, he's 30, with no kids. He would spend unwisely. He would buy like 5 pairs of the same shoe in different colors.
Yes, his spending was always out of control which was why we never had cable or electricity.

This brought to mind the memory of the time he found these red suede loafers that he thought were so cool and rich looking. They cost more than $100, and he bought three pairs in three different colors.

15k on his Jeep 10k in guns.
And also why he stole my identity and stole about $30k from me.
I wanted to go camping for my 30th bday. Something simple. He said he had saved to take me to Germany.

This was the international trip the doctor told me about. I realized she wasn't really having a conversation with me. I would write something, but she didn't respond, she just went on with her story. She was on autopilot and downloading. I was probably one of the few people she felt safe sharing her experience with. She didn't know me. She only knew that I knew the "real Stephen" and that was enough.

> *He told me he made $80k so I didn't question his high spending. I later found out on paper he made $45k. I had relocated back to Colorado because my grandma was dying. He was to look for a job and move here. Grandma passed and he came out for her funeral.*

Aww. Sorry to hear about your grandmother.

> *Two hours later we were still grieving at our home and the police came to arrest him.*

Oh woah....

> *I was yelling at the officer that they made a bad mistake. They said they had him on a felony count for $250k. Dr. Perelman called me and said there was a police sting.*

Geez, that must have been so scary. What did Stephen say?

> *And they had caught him on tape admitting to stealing from Dr. Perelman. I heard the audio almost 6 months after he passed. All the money, the Germany trip, his guns ... he took silver from his bosses safe. All stolen. The cops said they knew I was innocent. I was utterly in shock.*
>
> *The last time I saw him he was at court waiting for a decision to be extradited to Florida. He had his head bowed low and he'd lost about 20 pounds during those two weeks in jail. He could not look at me.*

I understood she couldn't answer my questions or have a real conversation about Stephen. She was still shattered. I remembered the shock I felt discovering all of the items he had purchased in my name. The shock of learning who he really was after we married. Even though he hadn't stolen from her yet, the façade had come crashing down in a sudden and dramatic way. I could imagine her disorientation and grief.

> *They drove him back to Florida, where he was released on bond. He was to live with his parents. He kept telling me he would prove his innocence.*
>
> *On Feb 25 he called me. Nothing strange in his voice. We spoke about my flying to see him, how the weather was still cold here.*
>
> *He said he was going on a hike. A couple of hours later messages came through on Facebook. "The password to my phone is ... the login to my laptop..." Then, a map of a park. Followed by a suicide note. I immediately called.*

OMG

> *Straight to voicemail. Called his mom, his dad, his aunt Deborah. I forwarded his family the email and said I felt Stephen was in grave danger. About an hour later I called back to the sound of Carol screaming. A team of*

police were at the park. Two hikers he said hello to on the way in called the police after hearing a gunshot. He sat on a bench I believe five miles back. Watched the sunset and shot himself in the head. With the last message to me saying I would be the last picture in his phone that he looked at. I didn't believe Dr. Perelman at first. I was angry. Traumatized. Confused.

I'm so sorry you had to go through that.

Reading her message, I was suddenly and deeply angry with Stephen again. With his last act, he chose to traumatize his girlfriend, someone he apparently loved. His message saying hers would be the last photo he would look at it seemed unbearably cruel ... and twisted.

Then I heard the police sting. It was true. I heard there were allegations of a stolen guitar from Musician Central, his previous employer. I just didn't think he was capable. He had an engagement ring in his pocket the night he was arrested. He was going to propose.

That's true; he stole a guitar for a girlfriend, according to mutual friends who work at Musician Central.

I try my best to remember the good memories.

It's definitely hard to be tricked that way.

I think he had an addictive personality and he had a lot of financial liberty with his boss. He lived with him on the water, got to take his Boston Whaler out when he wanted ... he got spoiled around money.

He was very good at getting people to trust him with important things.

And he took it too far. Dr. Perelman trusted him like a son. I don't think that makes him evil. I think that he had a problem. He would have done five years and could get help. Granted, I could not have stayed with him, but he didn't need to lose his life. Stealing isn't worthy of death. God would have had mercy on him.

No, he didn't need to die, for sure.

At this point I started to wonder if she truly understood what was happening. He was not facing five years. He had at least two charges against him and each carried a minimum sentence of five to ten years. I guess if he was only convicted of one charge and given the bare minimum, he could do five years. But the reality is he was probably facing at least ten years.

The confirmation for me was taking his life. If he wasn't guilty he wouldn't need to. He didn't want his parents or me to see him in that light ... to know the truth. I will always love him. Despite his actions.

You don't have to stop loving someone who was good to you because they made a mistake.

Fourteen. *The Girlfriend*

I felt like her last statement was almost an effort to seek validation for loving him or maybe just understanding. So I gave it to her. I was still reeling from his last message to her. She couldn't see the cruelty in it. To her, he was a tortured soul, in need of saving.

I was incredibly supportive when he was in jail. Once I started to suspect he was guilty, I became a bit distant as anyone would.

I'm glad that you have such good memories to look back on.

His parents said he died of a broken heart because he felt he couldn't be with me. Which I really struggled with. For them to place blame on me.

I thought back to his mother, looking at me in the backseat. "It's a woman's lot in life to suffer." I remembered how I took all the blame for the divorce, how everything was my responsibility. Now his family were still casting blame on everyone but Stephen. It had to be someone else's fault because it could never be Stephen's.

Yeah. His mom said that to me too, but I don't believe that. He would never go to jail and probably felt this was his only other option.

They cannot accept the truth, so I guess it's easier to say it's because he felt he couldn't be with me. I did what anyone who just found out the closest person in their life had lied extensively to them would do. When he knew I knew, he couldn't take it.

His parents have always struggled with who their son was. He abused me psychologically and physically. Every time I told them about it, they made excuses and told me "it was the woman's lot in life to suffer." They can't see the truth.

He never touched me physically. He would have met my dad's pistol.

Well, that stuff didn't happen until after we got married … he was a perfect gentleman until that.

She said, "He never touched me physically." Did that mean the yelling and games had started? James had mentioned that her family didn't like Stephen's "jokes." I had to guess that the emotional abuse had started. He wasn't able to hide who he was for long. But Angela was where I had been. She probably had no idea she was already in a cycle of abuse.

One thing I never understood was his cancer. He told me he had Non-Hodgkin's Lymphoma, not once, but twice. His parents never spoke about it. He never went into detail.

That's always been a question mark for me too…. I believe he never had cancer. I think he was doing drugs at the time of our divorce and he lost a lot of weight fast. The cancer was a lie to cover up the addiction. He disappeared for an entire year. I was the one who told his parents about the cancer. I heard about it and called his mom to offer support. But apparently at that time, they couldn't find him and had no idea.

He said he had it at 22. Were you with him then?

We got married when he was 22 and I was 20 ... and he did not have cancer. We were divorced by the time I was 26.

He told me he was married at 19.

"1/3/06 was our wedding date. He was 22 and turned 23 that December.

So he did steal from you?

I told her about his stealing my identity to finance things. The $30,000 worth of debt that I had no choice but to pay off myself. Always getting the mail and hiding everything from me. I wondered if she was putting things together. He stole from me, he stole from Musician Central, he stole from Dr. Perelman. Would he eventually have stolen from her? Had he stolen from her and she just didn't know it yet?

Yes. He had Dr. Perelman's mail hidden in bins.

In 2015 he emailed me asking for old tax returns for a business loan. He promised to give me money for the debt if I did. I had already paid it off. I knew he was a liar and I would never see any money, so I didn't send it. He told me he paid $750,000 for experimental cancer treatments and was cured of cancer within a year.

At this point she wasn't responding. I felt like maybe I told her too much. Maybe writing "I knew he was a liar" was too much reality. Maybe I sounded too angry for her. She was silent for a while, so I wrapped it up.

Sorry if you didn't want to know those things about him. Thanks for telling me your side of what happened. Hold the good memories!

And then she wrote:

He told me you guys had split because your parents were overbearing. But I never knew your name or anything about you.

Again with the lies about my parents!

No, we split because he was abusive and I caught him cheating. I moved into the spare bedroom and he came home drunk and assaulted me. When he passed out I grabbed what I could and left. He emptied our bank account twice. I was homeless, living in my car for two weeks until I could open my own account and get my direct deposit stopped. He had an employee who he was talking to at all hours of the night. I had gained weight during our marriage and he would rub this very skinny girl in my face and berate me, telling me how fat and worthless I was.

Wasn't he pretty overweight?

Fourteen. The Girlfriend

I noticed how she never offered sympathy or acknowledgment of my experience. It felt odd to me. Usually when you hear of someone's pain, you offer some sort of sympathy. But as I noticed before, we weren't having a real conversation. There was no back and forth. There was only her story and my story. To her, our stories had nothing in common. I understood it might take her years to understand how close she came to substantial danger.

He was overweight, but he thought he looked like Thor.

He told me he lost 100 pounds.

He didn't lose 100 pounds, maybe 40.

So what did James say? Same thing I said?

Pretty much, though he thought you two were broken up after the arrest. But he had experiences with Stephen, so he knew he wasn't a truthful person. He also said that Stephen complained about your parents a lot.

No. I stayed supportive until I knew for sure.

This was another moment where I felt like she was looking for validation from me. She felt guilty and wanted someone to tell her she did the right thing. This was Stephen's handiwork. He had left this woman feeling responsible for his death.

That's good. You can't always believe things at face value so I understand that.

I thought it was odd he didn't write his parents. He was close to them.

I wanted to tell her that he wasn't close to them, that if it wasn't for me, he would never have spoken to them during our marriage. I wanted to refer back to his disappearing for a year and not telling them that he had moved and been fired, but I didn't. I knew you couldn't break someone's chosen reality all at once. It was too much.

Yeah, it doesn't make sense. Of course, they told me there was no note.

He sent me a long note.

Maybe they didn't know about it?

"My grandma died and he was gone two weeks later. I forwarded them the note. They had it.

That's so tough. Ah, well, then I guess they lied for whatever reason.

We went through a rough patch the previous October. We didn't talk for over a month.

You and Stephen?

Stronger Than That

Yes. He created a fake dating profile and sent me a request. He denied it.
Oh wow … that's shady.

So the games had started. He would have loved catching someone flirting with a fake dating profile. It was the kind of trap he would set. Then he would have an excuse to blow up. He loved nothing more than a vortex of self-righteous anger. At this point it was way past my bedtime and she hadn't said anything for a while.

Well, I appreciate you chatting with me. I have to get to bed, but if you ever have any questions just reach out.

I waited a few minutes and there was no response, so I put the phone on the charger on the nightstand and fell asleep. When I woke up the next morning, I had messages waiting.

Thanks. Same.
Please don't tell his family I told you.

Hello?

I responded, "So sorry, I fell asleep. I won't tell his parents. I don't really talk to them anymore anyway."

There was no reply.

After this last interview I took some time to review all the versions of this story I had been told. It made me think of that movie where you see an event over and over but each time it is shown through the lens of a different witness to the event. Why are there so many versions? I blame it on one part trauma and one part revisionist history. Trauma can make you forget things in order to protect yourself (disassociation); it's not usually intentional. Revisionist history is something I became fascinated with while listening to all the versions of events and writing this book. Revisionist history, in my layperson description, is when we intentionally skew the facts of an event to make ourselves or others look better. It can be to protect ourselves from being seen in a poor light or it can be to protect ourselves from bad memories of someone. For Stephen's parents, I believe they decided to change the narrative because they didn't want people to think bad things about their son. Somewhere, in a blend of all the stories from people left in the wake of Stephen Jones, there is the truth.

Afterword

This book might make it seem like everything unfolded easily, chronologically, and rationally. It didn't work that way. I spent four years after my divorce fighting the memories. I tried to ignore it, power through it, just keep going through a sheer force of will. And I succeeded to a degree, but the unseen traps stored in my memory kept me from peace. Stephen's death brought some recollections to the surface, but it wasn't until I read Nick's article that I knew I was missing large parts of the puzzle. I started researching, reached out to people in Stephen's circle, and I hired an editing team. Sometimes we would just sit and talk while they asked me questions and pulled my story out of me. There was no judgment, no personal connection to my life, and something about that process released the grip on my mind. Often, I left those meetings, and later at night entire scenes from my life unfolded before me that I had completely locked away. I grabbed my laptop and wrote everything down before it slipped away from me once again.

I came to realize that there is a difference between "body memory" and "narrative memory." Memory issues are a symptom of PTSD. During my marriage, I experienced trauma, not just once or twice, but on a daily basis, over a six-year period. I suffered verbal and psychological abuse.

When I started writing, I was just throwing together a timeline of events so I wouldn't forget anything. At first, it felt like I remembered everything. As I started to expand upon the "events" to make them "stories," I found holes in my memory. Being unsure of the details started to make me question myself. Years of gaslighting caused me to doubt my perception of events. Was I making more out of things than they were? Sharing my experiences with my editors made me realize I was not crazy, and I was not "overreacting like I always do." Their reactions, both spoken and unspoken, reassured me.

Continuing to piece the stories together, I still couldn't remember details and I couldn't understand why. I told myself if things really happened this way, if it had been this bad, I would remember every disgusting detail. I turned to Google and typed in "Why can't I remember all the details of my abuse?" Thousands of results popped up. I found research abstracts and mainstream articles on "Memory Fragmentation and PTSD" and "Narrative Memory vs. Body Memory."

Have you ever instinctively ducked when someone raised a hand at you? This is body memory. You don't consciously go through an entire decision process to protect yourself from a slap. You have experienced this before (typically more than once) and now your body just takes over for you. With PTSD it may be triggered by someone using words you have heard before followed by "punishment" or it could be seeing one of those green four-door Jeep Wranglers that my ex used to drive. It's knowing something bad happened to you and not being able to articulate it.

I read about the concept that trauma isn't just in your head; it leaves a physical imprint on your body. There are three parts of the brain that on a brain scan can be seen as altered by trauma: The hippocampus shrinks—this is the center of emotion and memory; the amygdala function increases—the center of creativity and rumination; and the prefrontal/anterior cingulate function decreases—the center of more complex functions such as planning and self-development. Kind of like a computer virus in our brain, the unprocessed traumatic memories can become sticking points that cause our mental and physical processes to malfunction. Cellular/body memory seems to still be early in its research phase, but it shows that it's not just our brain but our body's cells that could hold an imprint of past traumatic events.

I read some articles that talked about a school of thought that getting people with PTSD to pull the pieces of these fragmented memories together can actually help them face and heal from them. This helped me understand why writing this book had such a positive effect on my healing process. I expected to be constantly triggered and to struggle with confronting the truth of what happened. I was surprised that for me the stories and memories no longer scared me. Am I "cured"? Not even close. I still randomly trigger sometimes, but I feel better equipped to quickly recognize that it's happening and then process it.

Gaslighting was part of my self-doubt and fuzzy memories. My abuser always worked to manipulate me into questioning myself and my sanity. Something was wrong with me and that's why he behaved the way he did. Every time he told me I couldn't take "a joke," or I was "too serious" and "overreacting," I believed him. Over the years I automatically minimized and ignored my own experiences and emotions. I was gaslighted this way for six years. It will take time for all of my memories to return. No one wakes up healed of the emotional scars overnight.

As I wrote this book, I saw in black and white all the times I questioned my own experience. Was this abuse? Was I in danger? Or was I overreacting? As I spoke to the other people in Stephen's orbit, I realized it was almost certain things would have escalated over time.

I read this quote recently: "leaving is a process, not an event." If you are in an abusive situation, you don't just walk out the door. Abusers use control and manipulation. You have to be strategic and plan this process carefully or your abuser might panic and try to hurt you or even kill you. Part of you might be nodding in recognition, or part of you might think this is hyperbole and I'm overstating it. I am not.

Familicide is when an offender kills or attempts to kill their current or former spouse/intimate partner and one or more of their biological children or stepchildren. Though there is not a great deal of research on familicides, what is known suggests it is almost always male violence against women.

Research suggests a history of domestic violence was identified in the majority of cases of familicide, but not always. A desire for and sense of entitlement to control is a more common denominator. Familicide often happens when the abuser loses control, especially when a victim either leaves or communicates a desire to leave the relationship.

You don't know how an abuser is going to react to ordinary events like leaving a window open or not having dinner ready on time. How is he going to react when you do the ultimate thing and leave? The most dangerous time in a relationship with an abuser is when you leave. You need a plan and must make sure you are doing it at the right time. I left in my car with a comforter and a week's worth of clothes and snuck back in the house every night for weeks to try and get clothes or my things. It was terrifying. But once I left, I got out and never looked back.

While I am certainly not suggesting that Stephen had the desire to kill me, or had planned to do so, I am suggesting that I feel lucky to have escaped my marriage alive.

So much of my life was psychological torture as I attempted to appease him and make him happy. I felt as if I were constantly trying to avoid punishment. If he wasn't happy by nighttime and we went to bed, if I even moved wrong, I was kicked and punched. If I left the bedroom and slept on the couch it would be even worse.

Afterword

You might still be in a stage where you're minimizing your abuse or rationalizing the behavior. I used to think, "He only hit me the one time...." Obviously, that is not true. There were many times he hit, kicked, and punched me in my sleep. And the times he pushed me on our way out the door and the times he threw things at me. Why didn't that register with me? I honestly never recognized it and kept repeating, "It was only the one time" until maybe three years after my divorce. I have spoken to other women who have gotten out of abusive relationships and found that most of them have a similar story. There was something that happened to them that in the moment they never recognized as abuse. Eventually, something clicks, but not until long after.

Over the years I have been in and out of therapy, one of the major things I struggled with is the idea that I must have done something to deserve what happened. I don't mean in some cosmic way; I mean in a "what did I do to make him so angry today?" kind of way. The process of writing this book and interviewing people who knew Stephen allowed me to see clearly there was nothing I could have done. No matter who Stephen was with, whether it was a business relationship or a new romantic relationship, abuse was going to happen. I didn't cause it by not being a good wife. Maybe you need to hear this as well.

After I left Stephen, dating was nearly impossible. Anything that reminded me of my time with Stephen caused me to react as if I'd touched a hot stove, even mundane things, like putting away groceries.

I wanted to have children in my 20s. Never did I imagine myself starting a family in my 30s. I was studying to be an opera singer when I met my ex-husband. I dropped all of that when he and I got married. So many things were sacrificed for that relationship. However, I am strong and independent, I have an MBA, I bought a house all on my own at 30, and I have an interesting career. Last year I married the love of my life, and this year we are welcoming our first child. I was so shy and reserved prior to my marriage and divorce. That is no longer the case. I love my friends and my family. I have a wonderful musical family and I am now a founding member of a professional ensemble and had my first paid soloist performance with a local orchestra. I am also very lucky to be in a loving relationship with a great man whom I appreciate more because of my past. None of these things would be true if I hadn't taken the path behind me. Of course, I would never have chosen to be abused, but I am comfortable with who I am right now.

I'm not surprised when people ask me if I hate him, but at this point, it feels like a far-away concept. No, I don't hate him ... now.

However, when I first left him, I was very angry, and I definitely hated him. I was disgusted by him, and I didn't want anything to do with him. I was surfing a wave of rage. It was almost like a high: once you're there you have to ride it until it goes away. I would go out with my girls and trash-talk him. Then I remembered really specific things about Stephen that helped feed my anger and I would focus on those.

One such thing was when I first met Stephen, he had long blond hair that was clean and always tied back in a low ponytail. He appeared to have good hygiene. After we married, I noticed his hygiene routine was non-existent. He never brushed his teeth. They were yellow and stained and he covered his bad breath with mints or gum. His gums were bright red and appeared swollen. One time, I got him to go to a dentist because he had a really bad toothache. He was popping Aleve for the pain like it was candy. At the dentist's office he was told he had severe gingivitis which was the cause of the red, swollen gums, and he had a badly infected and abscessed tooth in the back of his mouth that needed to be pulled. The dentist couldn't do the extraction because of the infection. He was put on antibiotics and given a time to go back for the procedure. He never went back. He didn't shower regularly so his blond hair was greasy and hung down in front of his face. He was always shaking his head to get his bangs out of his eyes. He would dress in nice jeans, stylish shoes, and cool t-shirts. On the surface, his vibe was cool hip musician, but if you got too close, you could see bad teeth and greasy hair and smell bad breath. I felt it was a perfect representation of him as a person. From a distance he was charming and well put together, but if you got too close, he was abusive and dirty.

I needed the anger for the first three months. It kept me going in the right direction: away from him! Dwelling on memories that fueled my disgust and rage felt necessary to keep me safe. But after a while, it felt like a storm was always brewing in my chest. I didn't like feeling that way. I had reached the point where it wasn't serving me anymore. With the help of a good therapist, I started to heal and forgive him. Not for his sake, but mine. Today, I am able to talk about him and feel nothing.

Once I was in my own apartment and the divorce papers were filed, I felt free, as if I had used that energy of anger and adrenaline to jump over tall walls. Now that I felt a little safer, it was time to let the anger go. This was hard because once I let go of the anger I was left with sadness and grief. Then I had to deal with the sense of failure. This is where the hopelessness kicks in and thoughts of suicide can creep their way into your mind. At least they did for me. Everyone has their own timeline. Some will need that rage to get through but some won't. For some, things will happen quickly; for others, things might take years. Everyone will handle things in their own way. There is no wrong way. There is only getting out and getting safe.

Sometimes I get asked how I feel about Stephen's death. This question is obviously specific to my situation, but everyone's experience will have strange twists and turns you couldn't previously imagine. My first reaction was shock and sadness; no matter what he did to me I never wished he would die. Maybe if he died in the first three months, I might have felt differently, but it had been two years and I had adjusted. It was just sad. I don't think anyone should take their own life. You make choices and you live with them. You steal and you do the time. But he had a different makeup than most people. For him, going to prison, being caught, and removing the mask 100 percent was not an option. I was devastated for his family.

However, I was relieved that I didn't have to always be looking over my shoulder. He was gone, so I didn't have to jump every time I saw a jeep that looked like his. I didn't have to worry it was him stalking me. Was he going to steal my identity again? Did he still have my Social Security number? Then, of course, I felt terrible and guilty that I felt relief. Was I a monster myself? But he had tormented me emotionally and physically. He would never be able to hurt anyone like that again.

If you're just getting out of a domestic violence situation, you might still be in shock. Parts of what you've been through may already be feeling unreal, as if it didn't happen to you. You might be surprised how it doesn't feel in the least "over." Again, every situation and person is different. But I can tell you what it was like for me.

For me it was all about taking Step 1, Step 2 and Step 3. I worked with a family member, and we figured out all of the steps together. I became very task oriented and driven during the time of my divorce. I was alone and all I knew was it needed to get done! So I started with a list of things that needed to happen and started executing those items. If I found I forgot something, I would have to re-adjust, or if I did something wrong, well, then, lesson learned and start over.

If and when you're ready to start sharing your story with people, you might hear something like "I thought you were stronger than that! How could you let this happen to you?" This question is like a gut punch. If someone says this to you, it's not true. You were stronger than that. You're here, you're not there, you're gone. I was tricked, manipulated, and fooled by someone but I kept up with his games and found my way out. For family members and people trying to help, this is one thing you should never say to someone getting out of an abusive situation.

It can be a challenge to talk about strength. Strength doesn't always look the same. I know that I have demonstrated my strength in many ways over the years. I think it's important for us to recognize strength in all its forms, not just for others but also for ourselves. I have felt weak and like a failure so many times. In the moment that was my truth, but when I look back, I can see a totally different story. I was strong while withstanding the abuse from my ex-husband; I thought I was weak taking all of this from him. Now that I understand what abuse is, I can see that it wasn't weakness but strength to survive. I tried to leave several times; that takes a lot of strength. It is so scary to try and leave a person like Stephen, and although not all attempts were successful, I eventually made it out. It's strong not to give up.

It takes an average of seven attempts for a victim of domestic abuse to leave successfully. Think about that. An average of seven means some can get out on the first try while others can get out on the fifteenth. It doesn't matter how many times you try; all that matters is that one of them will be successful. During various times, I knew that people in my life could not help me or handle knowing what was going on. At the time, I thought handling everything on my own, going it alone, was another form of strength. I made the conscious decision to shoulder the burden on my own. I didn't tell my parents the details about what was happening and never shared the details of the abuse after I was divorced. I didn't want them to feel guilt or pain that they should have done something when there was nothing they could have done until I was ready. Now, I understand that it would have been stronger to reach out for help. But I can't judge myself for thinking errors I had back then, or how I stayed, or how I left. Life is rarely by the book, always messy, and we do the best we can with the tools we have at the time. It's just funny to me now that I thought staying silent for so many years was the "strong" choice, and now here I am, writing it all in a book for the world to read!

I thought I was showing strength again when I decided not to tell his parents all the details of the abuse. This was their son. I told them just enough to make them understand that our marriage was beyond saving and no more. But by keeping that secret I was playing into the family's dynamic of hiding the truth, protecting the image of a perfect family, rather than allowing the reality to intrude. Now I understand that keeping the secrets of the abuser harms everyone. But at the time, it was what I was conditioned to do. Again, I can't judge myself for decisions I made in the maelstrom of confusion and pain.

It was hard, and I cried many nights while feeling the pressure of school, working full time, and going through the emotions of divorce. School really gave me something to focus on and it gave me a community. My MBA cohort was 25 women and two men. I had lots of female empowerment and support from my peers. When I finally finished in December of 2012 the moment was incomparable. That diploma meant something more to me than just the completion of a master's degree; it meant that I was not just surviving but I was thriving. I walked across the stage in my cap, gown and honor cords for finishing with a 4.0 GPA. I was handed my diploma and knelt as I received the hood that signified I have a master's. I looked out to the audience like all of the other graduates to see those there to support me, but I didn't have anyone in the crowd; I was doing this alone. In this moment I realized I was strong enough to support myself.

Common questions your close friends, family, and loved ones will ask are "Why didn't you tell someone while this was happening? Why didn't you come to me for help?" Your abuser teaches you shame, teaches you that you are not worthy, no one loves you, and no one cares. It's also embarrassing; you never know what people are going to say and how they are going to react. Your arguments with your significant other are different than mine. You can tell yours he or she is wrong without worrying about being emotionally tortured; you don't need to fear for your life. I would fear for my sanity and my life when I would stand up to Stephen. It's not the same as what is going on in the life of someone who doesn't have an abuser. To me, a big red flag is someone who never complains about his or her spouse.

Some people might want to retroactively "fix" your marriage or relationship, so you'll get questions like "Did you try couples therapy?" People think that before you "give up" on marriage you should try everything, but when you're in a relationship with an abuser, he or she isn't going to therapy. In fact, your abuser isn't going to let you go because he or she might get outed. And even if your abuser does agree to go, it could be extremely dangerous; you might say something in what is a safe space, but then you have to go home and who knows what will happen then? Even when talking to a therapist you would probably just be sugarcoating things. Again, I try to remind myself that most people only have non-abusive relationships in their histories. The possibilities and solutions that are available in a healthy relationship are often dangerous in an abusive one.

Stephen was my first real relationship and the only man I had ever slept with at this point. I was terrified of putting myself out there. Dating apps were just becoming popular, so I found one of the free apps and tried to start dating. Once I got a little braver, I would move to texting with a guy. I started to find myself on the apps all day. I was getting all of the things I had never gotten from my husband. Men told me I was pretty or sexy. Me? Pretty? I was so naïve that I assumed all of them were sincere in what they were saying to me. I had been starved for positive attention for so long that it was easy to become addicted to the apps. I started what I will call "serial dating"—a lot of first dates but hardly any second dates. I quickly realized on these dates that most of the guys just wanted sex.

Eventually I met a guy who was so completely the opposite of my ex-husband and I was instantly drawn to him. He was a giant teddy bear. He was very simple and was damaged like me. He told me about how his last girlfriend was emotionally abusive to him. My judgment was clouded in this relationship; he was so sweet and kind to me that I did everything to make it work. He didn't have any money. I was making good money with my recent promotion and so I financed every date. I overlooked the fact that he was in his late 20s and still living at home. I brought him back to Maine with me and introduced him to my parents, and my dad got him a job working for the shipyard where he worked. Things were going so well. We had careers we loved, we bought a house together, and we got engaged on our one-year anniversary.

However, I was struggling with PTSD. Living with someone after the type of marriage I had was difficult. I was always afraid to upset him. The first time he did laundry and saw something of mine on the floor in the bedroom, he asked if it was dirty and needed to be washed. I remember vividly being downstairs and looking up at him, feeling panicked. "Yes, I'll take care of it," I said frantically as I went running up the stairs. I reacted in the way I had been conditioned for so many years. My body knew that if he had to clean up after me, I was going to be in trouble later. It was the same with dishes. If I cooked, he wanted to help do the dishes after, and it took a long time for me to feel comfortable with the help. It would stress me out so much, just the anticipation of punishment for not doing everything myself.

The relationship eventually ended badly. I was so focused on all the ways he was different from my ex and trying to prove that I was a good partner and would be a good wife that I missed all the things happening right under my nose—affairs with eight different women. It could have been more, but I stopped looking after eight. I could write a second book just about the bad relationships over the five years after this break up until I found my true soulmate and now husband.

I would say intellectually, it wasn't hard for me to trust again. I am the type of person who thinks people are basically good. But my body was on high alert for years, waiting for the other shoe to drop. I struggled with intimacy or people getting in my space. Due to Stephen's punching and kicking me during the night, I cannot sleep if someone is touching me. I get very anxious that if I move it will disturb him and he will get angry. I would break up with people because they wanted to cuddle. I had to make a choice; don't tell the guy I can't sleep if I'm being touched and then stay awake with anxiety the whole night while he tries to spoon or introduce the awkward conversation "I have PTSD due to surviving domestic abuse." It was easier to just end the relationship.

Later I learned I could be honest and tell people I have PTSD and can't be touched when I sleep. Over the years, I've regained my ability to trust with my whole heart, but I don't have any tolerance for bullshit anymore. On our first date, I told my husband, "I am not here to impress you."

Healing happens in waves. Even now, things come up in life, and when I pull back the curtain, there is Stephen. In order to survive physically and psychologically, we adapt to our abuser. Those survival strategies don't work in the real world. A few years ago, I was at a manager's retreat. I work in a male dominated field. Halfway through the night, I was at a big round table with a bunch of men. The man to my right put his hand on my leg. I thought to myself, "Maybe he doesn't realize that's not his leg?" So I moved my leg. But no, the hand came back. I twisted farther away from him. And once again, the hand was there. I asked him about his family, his wife and his kids, and I mentioned my fiancé. Nothing was working.

Finally, I figured he wasn't going to stop and I may as well cut my evening short. He followed me to the elevator. I asked him which floor he was going to, but he didn't say anything. When I pushed the button for my floor he said, "That works." Now I was scared. My palms were sweating, and I stared straight ahead. The second the doors opened I literally ran down the hall to my room, praying I could get my door open quickly. I must have looked like a crazy person, but I felt the most overwhelming fear.

Now I realize that I did everything but say out loud, "Hey, buddy, that's not your leg." The thing is, in my world with Stephen, confrontation of any kind was dangerous. Speaking that way still felt dangerous. I realized that at times I've learned to avoid any confrontation even when it's necessary. This leads to all kinds of problems. But I'm aware of it now, and that's part of the healing process.

As I write this it is January 2022. The world feels like it is off its axis. Between the Covid-19 pandemic and the political unrest, even the sanest person is feeling vulnerable and stressed. Now I think about a person who is an abuser. Did he lose his job during the pandemic? Is he stuck working from home, with no outlet for any of his aggressive tendencies? Is he now home 24/7 with his wife and their kids who are unable to attend school in person and are now being "home schooled"? This is a dangerous time for victims of domestic abuse. A simple Google search will produce article after article from all over the world saying things like "DV incidents have tripled in 2020 compared to 2019." These numbers are horrifying. There is no perfect solution. My suggestion is, if you suspect someone may be at risk, call them. Keep in contact but keep in mind that they may not be alone; the abuser is probably standing right there. Coming right out and asking via text may not be a good idea as the abuser will probably be able to see the phone at some point. Always ask if they are alone before asking any direct questions. You can also reach out to a local DV advocacy group or call a hotline to ask for advice.

Lastly, it was important for me to remember that I was not alone. I was not the only person who had these doubts and feelings. I hope that through reading this book you will start to know that you are not alone either. I am right here with you, daily working through recovery. We are stronger than that.

Index